LEARNING THEORIES

FOR
EARLY YEARS PRACTICE

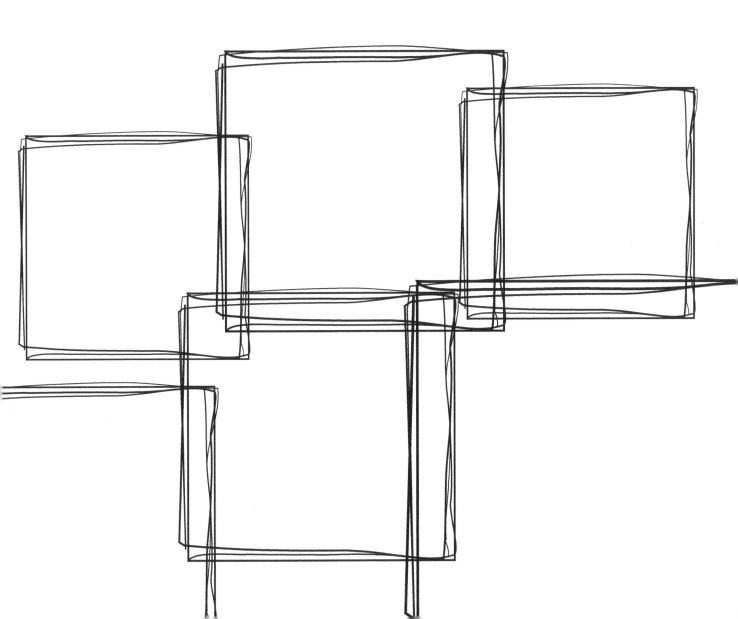

LEARNING THEORIES

FOR
EARLY YEARS
PRACTICE

SEAN MACBLAIN

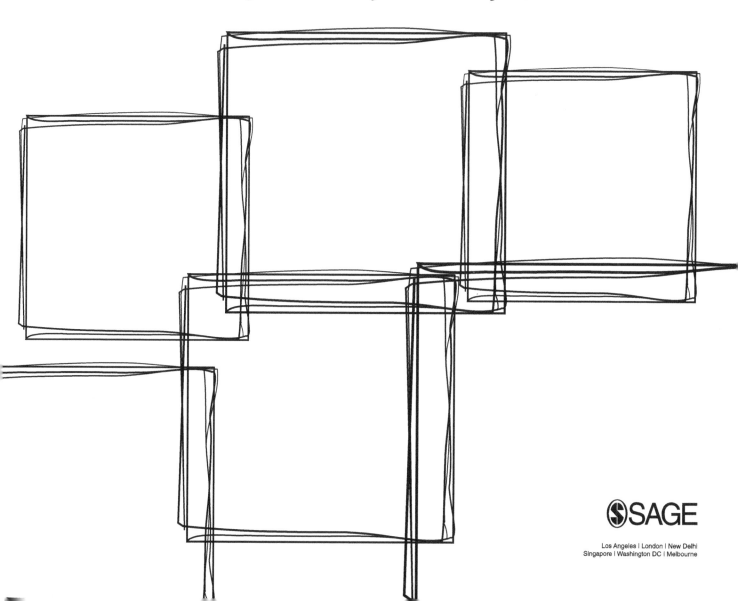

$SAGE

Los Angeles | London | New Delhi
Singapore | Washington DC | Melbourne

Los Angeles | London | New Delhi
Singapore | Washington DC | Melbourne

SAGE Publications Ltd
1 Oliver's Yard
55 City Road
London EC1Y 1SP

SAGE Publications Inc.
2455 Teller Road
Thousand Oaks, California 91320

SAGE Publications India Pvt Ltd
B 1/I 1 Mohan Cooperative Industrial Area
Mathura Road
New Delhi 110 044

SAGE Publications Asia-Pacific Pte Ltd
3 Church Street
#10-04 Samsung Hub
Singapore 049483

Editor: Jude Bowen
Editorial assistant: Catriona McMullen
Production editor: Victoria Nicholas
Copyeditor: Sharon Cawood
Proofreader: Elaine Leek
Marketing manager: Dilhara Attygalle
Cover design: Wendy Scott
Typeset by C&M Digitals (P) Ltd, Chennai, India
Printed in the UK

Library of Congress Control Number: 2017953949

British Library Cataloguing in Publication data

A catalogue record for this book is available from
the British Library

ISBN 978-1-5264-3208-7
ISBN 978-1-5264-3209-4 (pbk)

At SAGE we take sustainability seriously. Most of our products are printed in the UK using responsibly sourced papers
and boards. When we print overseas we ensure sustainable papers are used as measured by the PREPS grading
system. We undertake an annual audit to monitor our sustainability.

For all our children

ACKNOWLEDGEMENTS

I would like to offer my sincere thanks to Jude Bowen who was encouraging from the outset and who allowed the idea for this text to take shape. My thanks must also go to Catriona McMullen who, throughout the whole process, has been most helpful and supportive. I would also like to acknowledge the support I received from the following highly experienced and expert staff at two wonderful early years settings:

- Alison Blasdale and Lucy Smith at Millfield Pre-Prep:
  https://millfieldschool.com/pre-prep
- Holly Bowman and Claire Hooker at Emneth Nursery School and Children's Centre:
  www.emneth-nur.norfolk.sch.uk

I would also like to acknowledge the support of my dear friend Barbara Hendon, a specialist in the field of early years who, over the years, has been a wonderful source of information and inspiration. Finally, I would like to thank my wife, Angela, for her continued support throughout writing this book.

CONTENTS

ABOUT THE AUTHOR

Sean MacBlain PhD is a distinguished author and academic whose publications include: MacBlain (Sage, 2014) *How Children Learn*; Gray and MacBlain (Sage, 2015) *Learning Theories in Childhood*, now going into its 3rd edition; MacBlain, Long and Dunn, (Sage, 2015) *Dyslexia, Literacy and Inclusion: Child-centred Perspectives*; MacBlain, Dunn and Luke (Sage, 2017) *Contemporary Childhood*. Sean's publications are used by students, academics and practitioners worldwide. Sean is currently a senior academic at Plymouth Marjon University where he previously held the positions of Research Lead for the Centre for Professional and Educational Research, Research Coordinator for the School of Education and Deputy Chair of the Ethics Committee. Sean also worked previously as a Senior Lecturer in Education and Developmental Psychology at Stranmillis University College, Queens University Belfast. In addition to this, Sean has also worked for over twenty years as an educational psychologist and continues in this field as an independent practitioner. Sean is married to Angela and lives in Somerset, England.

FOREWORD

As a teacher educator, I am often confronted with a response of apathy when I introduce students, particularly those in the initial years of their degree programme, to any form of theoretical issue or philosophical debate. Familiar comments include: 'But why do we need to know something that happened 100 years ago?' or 'it is only when I am in the classroom that I really learn – all this theoretical stuff is just a waste of time'. These students appear only interested in the everyday practices of the classroom context and fail to appreciate what this book (entitled *Learning Theories for Early Years Practice*) is all about, i.e. we need to look at notable philosophies and theorists to help us unravel and deconstruct our own understandings of what good early years practice entails. As McMillan (2009) argues, an ability to reflect on appropriate theories is essential to equip students to become competent professionals who can engage with complex early years issues. Failing to embrace these theoretical issues may result in what could be described as narrow and shallow perceptions of what constitutes high quality practice in the early years of education, which Walsh (2017) suggests will do little to address the real learning needs and interests of the young child.

As the opening chapter of this book aptly reminds us, the early years of education are often characterized as sugar and spice and all things nice, where 'each day is filled with the joys of seeing young minds develop', bringing with it 'lots of fun and immeasurable satisfaction' where early years practitioners are 'tasked daily with finding new and exciting ways of developing young children's thinking and learning'. Such a description of early years education certainly confirms why 'being a practitioner in early years settings is surely one of the most rewarding and satisfying jobs', as the author of *Learning Theories for Early Years Practice* clearly articulates in his final paragraph of the concluding chapter. Yet with such a mental image often comes a misapprehension that no particular skills, understanding or professional knowledge may be needed on the part of the early years teacher to fulfil the requirements of such a role, and on occasions can result in a disparaging attitude towards early years professionalism (McMillan, 2017). It is for this reason that the book in question is so timely. The author makes no excuse for suggesting that working in the early years can be an extremely worthwhile, satisfying and challenging experience but he makes it perfectly clear that a rich theoretical underpinning and a rigorous conceptual understanding are required to teach effectively in an early years setting, reinforcing the need for a 'professional not an amateur' (McMillan, 2017, p. 204). Tapping into a book which provides students and existing early years practitioners with a plethora of theories, both historical and more modern, alongside a clear application to everyday practice, has not been easy to find on our library shelves and I have no difficulty in saying that *Learning Theories for Early Years Practice* definitely fills this gap.

What makes this book stand out from the rest is not only the detailed and rich text which draws together an array of familiar and not so familiar theories on early years education, but also the clear structure and complementary features which make the text so appropriate, in particular for a student audience. The book is divided into three parts, namely Early Influences, Modern Influences and Challenges for Theorists in a Changing World. Parts 1 and 2 follow an identical structure where the reader is first introduced to a background synopsis on the theorist and then an attempt is made to help the reader understand the theory more fully. The reader then moves on to address what the theory really looks like in practice, drawing on examples from the early years context. Strengths and weaknesses of the theories are then considered and links to other theories are highlighted. Complementary features include selected activities, often online, discussion points and recommended readings, making the text a truly interactive experience. In this way, the book is not simply a narrative of theoretical content, but also ensures that theories are made real in the 21st century and in an early years context.

In summary, this is certainly a comprehensive and thought-provoking text, which provides a rich analysis of past and present theories and philosophies, informing the phase we know as early childhood education. Yet I would argue that this text does even more, where the final section goes one step further by challenging existing theories in an ever-changing landscape – a complex landscape where the true essence of childhood, and in particular young children's learning and development, have become subservient to issues concerning children's health, well-being and general safety. In my opinion, this book is a must read for all those interested in early childhood education. Those who never really understood the value of theory for ECE cannot help but do so after reading this book. Enjoy!

Glenda Walsh, Head of Early Years Education,
Stranmillis University College

REFERENCES

McMillan, D. (2009) 'Preparing for educare: student perspectives on early years training in Northern Ireland', *International Journal of Early Years Education*, 17(3): 219–35.

McMillan, D. (2017) 'Towards the playful professional', in G. Walsh, D. McMillan and C. McGuinness (eds), *Playful Teaching and Learning* (pp. 198–212). London: Sage.

Walsh, G. (2017) 'Why playful teaching and learning?', in G. Walsh, D. McMillan and C. McGuinness (eds), *Playful Teaching and Learning* (pp. 7–20). London: Sage.

INTRODUCTION

There can be few jobs as rewarding as working in an early years setting. Each day is filled with the joys of seeing young minds develop and the challenges of applying one's own knowledge and skills to finding new ways of facilitating and extending children's thinking and learning. In recent years, there has been an explosion in our knowledge of children's development in the early years and a significant growth in our understanding of how young children learn. Colleges and universities now offer new and exciting courses and programmes for students and prospective practitioners, which are organized and delivered by highly experienced staff with a wealth of expertise. Two decades ago, I (the author) was fortunate to be lecturing at Bridgwater College in Somerset, UK when colleagues at the college first introduced the concept of 'Forest Schools'. At the time, it was a joy to observe my colleagues' enthusiasm as they introduced this new concept of Forest School within the Children's Centre, following their visits to Scandinavia. Having also worked as an educational psychologist across a wide range of early years settings, I fully appreciated the benefits that Forest Schools could offer to all young children. My work as a psychologist also permitted me to see, at first hand, the extremely valuable and informed practice that takes place every day within the early years sector.

ABOUT THIS BOOK

In early years settings, every day is different and brings with it new challenges, lots of fun and immeasurable satisfaction at seeing young children grow and develop through a host of activities at the heart of which is 'language' and 'play'. Practitioners find themselves tasked daily with exploring new and exciting ways of developing children's thinking, their social and emotional development, and supporting them as they progress through the years towards formal education.

Why children learn in the way they do has exercised thinking for generations. We are still not entirely clear as to how children learn and what activities bring about

Our understanding of children's learning is now far more advanced than ever before

the best learning outcomes. How, for example, do we know when learning is taking place and what exactly do we understand by the term 'learning'? It is important to emphasize that learning is not just the act of acquiring new information and knowledge within classrooms; learning is far more complex than that. Jarvis (2005, pp. 2–3), for example, has emphasized the extremely complex nature of learning, asking if we should aim to understand learning 'as a set of cognitive mechanisms or rather as an emotional, social and motivational experience ... What should be the focus of learning, facts or skills?'

To help us understand how children learn, we need to look at what notable philosophers and theorists have proposed is good practice. Understanding what is meant by philosophy and by theory is, however, not straightforward and though the work of practitioners is informed to varying degrees by different philosophies and theories, confusion still surrounds the question of what exactly philosophy and theory are. In a lighthearted and tongue-in-cheek way, the philosopher De Botton (2000, p. 205) cited one of the most renowned philosophers, Friedrich Nietzsche, who suggested that 'the majority of philosophers have always been "cabbage-heads"'. De Botton, however, has also proposed that philosophers can show us what we feel and perhaps, more importantly, 'give shape to aspects of our lives that we recognise as our own, yet could never have understood so clearly on our own' (p. 9). What De Botton is suggesting here is that philosophers provide us with a means by which we can more fully understand how we think and why we do what we do.

Theory, on the other hand, has been well explained by Newby (2010, p. 71) who drew an important distinction between *education theory*, which deals with such areas as learning and child development, schooling and curricula, and *research theory*, which specifies procedures. Newby proposed how education theory can shape our understanding of learning and provide us with a means through which we can make more informed decisions. In contrast, he also proposed how research theory 'is a rule book whose legitimacy stems from principles accepted by the academic community and whose coherence owes much to custom and practice'.

Though philosophers and theorists have attempted to explain learning in different ways, they have also demonstrated many similarities; how learning takes place and which practice by adults offers the best outcomes; and which type of environmental factors support effective learning. Each theory, though different, has added significantly to how we make sense of children's learning. In their simplest form, theories are ways of explaining the complex nature of phenomena that we do not fully understand and phenomena that occur within ever shifting historical, economic and political contexts.

It is also important to understand that theorists, like philosophers, are influenced by the worlds they are born into and the events that take place around them. Importantly, they are also influenced by their own unique and personal histories and life experiences when growing up. It is interesting, for example, how some theorists and philosophers who dedicated much of their lives to understanding and explaining children's learning, experienced significant trauma in their own early lives. Friedrich Froebel, for example, experienced the death of his mother only nine months after his birth and received virtually no emotional support from adults until the age of 10 years when he went to live with his uncle, a caring and affectionate person who provided

Friedrich with the sense of security that had been lost to him after the death of his mother. Similarly, the philosopher Jean-Jacques Rousseau also lost his mother in early childhood; he was only nine days old at the time. By the age of 10, Jean-Jacques had experienced further separation and emotional upheaval when his father moved away from the family home, leaving Jean-Jacques to be reared by relatives. Johann Pestalozzi lost his father when he was 5 years of age and Rachel and Margaret McMillan, born respectively in 1859 and 1860, lost their father and their sister Elizabeth in 1865 when they were both still children.

The theorist John Dewey was born less than a year after his parents had experienced the death of his older brother, and the noted behaviourist Burrhus Skinner experienced emotional tragedy when his brother Edward, who was just two and a half years younger than him, died at age 16. The noted educationalist and psychoanalyst Susan Isaacs, who is known for developing nursery schools, also lost her mother when still a child. Such tragedies in the lives of these early philosophers and theorists must certainly have influenced their views of childhood and may have shaped within them a desire to devote their lives to understanding and improving the lives of young children. It is also notable, for example, that Jerome Bruner, whose ideas on education and learning still influence much practice today, was born blind (due to cataracts), a fact that must have weighed heavily on how he was parented as a young child.

AIMS OF THE BOOK

Understanding and applying learning theories are crucial to any transition from being a student to actual practice in real-life settings. This book aims to prepare the reader for practice in early years settings with children aged 0 to 5 years, by demonstrating how key learning theories underpin practice; readers will be supported in this process by photographs and examples of learning activities with clear explanations.

Divided into three main sections, *Early Influences*, *Modern Influences*, and *Challenges for Theorists in a Changing World*, the book identifies key theorists in early childhood, past and present, before

Applying theory to practice helps us understand the beginnings of learning in each child

Children respond positively to challenges in stimulating environments

linking them to a range of important issues that face early years practitioners today. Explanations of each theorist are guided by a clear structure, including: 'Links to other theorists'; 'Strengths and weaknesses of the theory'; and 'Theories in practice'. In addition, the book offers readers many case studies, activities and points for discussion; extended and recommended readings are also included and offer a highly valuable resource for students as well as their tutors.

EARLY YEARS PRACTICE IN CONTEXT

In addition to understanding how theorists and philosophers' own lives might have impacted on their thinking, it is important also to recognize that practice in the early years has been greatly influenced by political decisions. Practice in early years in the UK has been significantly impacted on by some important initiatives, which, though having their origins in theory, grew from directions adopted by successive governments. Four such initiatives are: *HighScope*, *Sure Start and the growth of Children's Centres*, and the *Statutory Framework for the Early Years Foundation Stage* and the *Integrated Review at 2 to 2½*.

HIGHSCOPE

Although originally developed in Michigan in the USA, *HighScope* has come to influence practice in the UK and throughout the world. Drawing initially on the work of Jean Piaget and John Dewey, *HighScope* has also drawn on other theorists such as Lev Vygotsky and Jerome Bruner and, more recently, academics researching children's learning. Within the UK, many of the principles of *HighScope* have been employed across many sections of the education system. It is used, for example, to address the needs of children with additional needs and those children who have been recognized as vulnerable. As with other approaches, *HighScope* seeks to support young children in building their knowledge and skills and in gaining much better understanding of their environments, their cultures and the communities and societies into which they are born. Central to the *HighScope* approach is the idea that learning is a process in which children should actively engage and that *High Scope* practitioners become as active as the children they are working with. The *HighScope* approach also 'promotes independence, curiosity, decision-making, co-operation, persistence, creativity', in addition to 'problem solving' (Miller and Pound, 2011, p. 103). Such principles are now fully endorsed by most early years practitioners and primary teachers as being central to their practice. (Take time to view the following URL link: https://highscope.org, which offers a wealth of information and material on *HighScope*.) Similar to *HighScope* is 'Sure Start'.

SURE START AND THE GROWTH OF CHILDREN'S CENTRES

The *Sure Start* initiative, which introduced 'Sure Start Local Programmes' in 1998 in the UK, was brought about largely by the then Chancellor of the Exchequer, Gordon Brown, under a Labour government. Though originally aimed at young children and families in England, other regions across the UK – Wales, Scotland and Northern Ireland – also embraced this initiative and adapted the underlying principles to serve their own areas. The initiative had its origins in a range of political factors within the UK, perhaps most notably a commitment by government to tackle poverty. It was also influenced by similar initiatives in the USA – the US 'Head Start' programme had been running since the mid-1960s and had been developed to provide support for pre-school children of low-income families; and, more recently, the 'Early Head Start' programme extended support for children from birth to 3 years and, importantly, support for pregnant mothers.

Sure Start was introduced with the intention of providing those children who most needed it with a much better start in their early years, which would benefit them as they progressed through childhood and into adulthood. At the time, the then Labour government had demonstrated a huge commitment to tackling poverty in the UK and saw supporting children in their first years as well as their families as key to improving society in general. Targeted improvements for supporting families with childcare were viewed as important, as was the need to improve the health of many children and implement measures that would improve their well-being. In addition to this, it was recognized that support was needed to develop those poorer and more disadvantaged communities into which many children were being born and spending

their first years. The level of funding given for this initiative was, at the time, considerable, being around £540 million between 1999 and 2002. It had been estimated that around 150,000 children who were living in relative deprivation would benefit from Sure Start. Though the government at the time agreed to provide funding for 10 years, the Chancellor reported in 2003 that responsibility for Sure Start would be relocated to local government by 2005, with the aim of establishing Sure Start centres in every community that needed it.

Following 2003, 'Sure Start Local Programmes', in addition to some nurseries and other pre-school provision, came under the umbrella term, *Sure Start Children's Centres* (SSCCs), with centres increasingly appearing across the UK. In 2011 there were, for example, nearly 4000 centres. Cuts in budgets, however, resulting from austerity measures brought about by more recent governments, have resulted

in the closure of many centres, with some centres having to merge and manage with limited staff. Indeed, Fitzgerald and Kay (2016, pp. 43–4) commented recently on how over half of day care places were lost when the previous Coalition government withdrew the legal requirement for SSCCs to provide this service, despite a growth in usage by parents, with an increase of 50,000 from 2013–2014 to reach 1.05 million. They also drew attention to the fact that estimates for cuts in budgets to SSCCs have been around 35 per cent since 2010.

Fitzgerald and Kay (2016, p. 43) recently reported findings from the National Audit Office published in 2006, who, in evaluating SSCCs, found that the majority of families were pleased with the services on offer. They also indicated how fathers and ethnic minority groups, in addition to families of children with disabilities and those with the 'highest level of difficulty', were failing to have their needs met by centres. Fitzgerald and Kay also indicated how some centres had not developed working relationships with health services that were effective.

Ofsted (2006, 2008) has drawn attention to the strengths and weaknesses of SSCCs, highlighting the need for local authorities to monitor their effectiveness, how they are managed and to engage in a process of evaluating outcomes for children and their families. Ofsted has also raised the issue of how the coordination of services, accessed by some centres, had not always been undertaken efficiently, in addition to the fact that some family 'types' were not availing themselves of what was on offer at the centres.

It is possible to locate the ideas that underpin *Sure Start* in the ideas of many of the theorists covered in this book. Pestalozzi, for example, grew up in poverty and recognized the importance of education as a means of supporting very young children and their families. Similarly, John Dewey and Bronfenbrenner recognized how the communities and cultures into which children were born and developed impacted significantly on their learning and development, and also on how children would, in turn, become active and purposeful members of their societies, a view that also lay at the very heart of Rousseau's philosophy.

STATUTORY FRAMEWORK FOR THE EARLY YEARS FOUNDATION STAGE

On 1 September 2012, the *Statutory Framework for the Early Years Foundation Stage* became mandatory in England for all early years providers in maintained and non-maintained schools, and independent schools as well as all providers on the *Early Years Register*, though it was recognized that there might be some exemptions to this final group. Though the Framework has been superseded by the more recent EYFS *Statutory Framework for the Early Years Foundation Stage: Setting the Standards for Learning, Development and Care for Children from Birth to Five* (2014) and '*Revised EYFS Framework 2017*' (see www.foundationyears.org.uk/eyfs-statutory-framework – accessed 07.08.17), it is worth exploring the 2012 Framework in some detail for it is in this document that we find the key thinking behind much current practice.

Children's minds are open to learning from the 'very start'

The quality of creative experiences in the first years adds hugely to children's learning

The new Framework built on existing practice, with the vision being that 'every child deserves the best possible start in life and the support that enables them to fulfil their potential' (DfE, 2012, p. 2; revised 2014). The Early Years Foundation Stage (EYFS) Framework recognized that development in children nowadays is quicker than in previous generations and that children's life experiences after birth and up to the time they begin formal schooling at 5 years of age are crucially important and have a significant influence on their later lives. Of particular importance to practitioners was the fact that Ofsted would inspect the implementation and application of the new Framework and provide reports on the quality and standards of provision inspected with their reports being published; in some instances, Ofsted might issue a 'notice to improve' or a 'welfare requirements notice'. Providers who failed to comply with a 'welfare requirements notice' would be deemed as committing an offence.

The *Statutory Framework for the Early Years Foundation Stage* proposed four overarching principles, which should be central to practice in early years settings:

- every child is a **unique child**, who is constantly learning and can be resilient, capable, confident and self-assured [Readers should refer to the section on developing emotional intelligence where the concept of resilience is more fully explored]

- children learn to be strong and independent through **positive relationships**
- children learn and develop well in **enabling environments**, in which their experiences respond to their individual needs and there is a strong partnership between practitioners and parents and/or carers
- **children develop and learn in different ways and at different rates**. (DfE, 2012, p. 3)

The Framework also proposed seven key areas crucial to learning and development in young children: communication and language; physical development; personal, social and emotional development; literacy; mathematics; understanding the world; and expressive arts and design. MacBlain et al. (2017, p. 23) explained these as follows:

The first three of these were to be viewed as 'Prime' areas, which would be particularly crucial, with the next four being seen as 'Specific' areas, which providers should take close account of in supporting children with the development of the Prime areas. The Framework stressed the importance of providers paying particular attention to the individual needs of children, in addition to the stage of development at which children are perceived to be functioning. With the introduction of the Framework, particular attention was to be given to the Prime areas, and especially when managing the learning experiences of very young children, which, the Framework proposed, 'reflect the key skills and capacities all children need to develop and learn effectively, and become ready for school'. (DfE, 2012, p. 6)

The Framework also placed emphasis on the importance of assessment:

Ongoing assessment (also known as formative assessment) is an integral part of the learning and development process. It involves practitioners observing children to understand their level of achievement, interests and learning styles, and to then shape learning experiences for each child reflecting those observations. (DfE, 2012, p. 10) and emphasized how:

> Assessment should not entail prolonged breaks from interaction with children, nor require excessive paperwork. Paperwork should be limited to that which is absolutely necessary to promote children's successful learning and development. (DfE, 2012, p. 10)

The Framework also placed emphasis on two areas: child protection, stressing that 'providers must have and implement a policy, and procedures, to safeguard children' (p. 13); and the importance of training and qualifications for those working with young children.

THE INTEGRATED REVIEW AT 2 TO 2½

The UK Department of Health (DoH) recently commissioned the National Children's Bureau (NCB, 2015) to undertake a review of early childhood with the purpose of identifying children's progress at age 2 to 2½ as a means of promoting more positive outcomes for them when they were older regarding their health and well-being, and learning and behaviour. A key rationale behind this review was to change how many adults think about young children's early development and to bring about improved practice.

Each child's capacity for learning in their first years is truly remarkable

The review was introduced alongside the 'Health Visitor Implementation Plan' (see www.gov.uk/government/publications/health-visitor-implementation-plan-2011-to-2015) – a four-year-long initiative focusing on greater recruitment and retention of health visitors and promotion of their continuing professional development. In addition, far greater entitlement to free early education for 2-year-olds was proposed. From September 2010, every 3- and 4-year-old had, for example, become entitled to 15 hours per week of funded early education. This was subsequently increased to include 2-year-old children considered to be disadvantaged. This entitlement was phased in gradually, with around 20 per cent of 2-year-olds becoming eligible by September 2013 and some 40 per cent eligible a year later, in September 2014. The increase in children attending early years settings would then, it was proposed, result in more children benefitting from an integrated review that would have an increased focus on health as well as learning.

Importantly, it was also proposed that assessments of children's public health would take place and would then inform decisions regarding the funding and shaping of services for young children and their families. It was proposed, for example, that data would be gathered through the *Integrated Review*, in addition to the *Healthy Child Programme Review* (www.gov.uk/government/publications/healthy-child-programme-rapid-review-to-update-evidence), also at 2 years of age for children who are not in early education. Questionnaires were to be completed by parents along with their health visitors and focus on the following key elements: *communication*, *gross* and *fine motor coordination*, *problem solving*, and *personal* and *social development*. In October 2015, responsibility for commissioning public health services for children aged 0–5 including health visiting was transferred to local authorities, which included the *Healthy Child Programme* and the *Integrated Review*. It was of note that whilst health visitors should continue being employed by their providers (mostly the NHS), responsibility for planning and payment of services would lie with local authorities (see the Kings Fund website for information relating to the new NHS health and well-being boards at: www.kingsfund.org.uk/projects/new-nhs/health-and-wellbeing-boards).

Key to the thinking behind these recent initiatives has been an increased acknowledgement that learning and development in the early years are rapid

Timeline

1632	John Locke is born
1712	Jean-Jacques Rousseau is born
1723	Poaching becomes a capital offence and those caught may be hanged
1745	Jacobite rising in Scotland led by Bonnie Prince Charlie ends with battle of Culloden
1746	Johann Pestalozzi is born
1782	Friedrich Froebel is born
1837	Queen Victoria comes to the throne
1840	Vaccination for the poor is introduced in England
1845	Irish potato famine begins with an estimated one million adults and children dying
1854	Crimean War begins
1856	Sigmund Freud is born
1859	John Dewey and Rachel McMillan are born
1860	Margaret McMillan is born
1861	Rudolf Steiner is born; the American Civil War begins
1865	President Lincoln is assassinated
1870	Maria Montessori is born; Charles Dickens dies
1880	Education becomes compulsory in England for children under 10 years of age
1888	Jack the Ripper begins his serial murders in London
1896	Piaget and Vygotsky are born; Bridget Driscoll becomes the first person in the world to be killed in a motor accident in London
1904	Burrhus Skinner is born
1914	World War I breaks out
1915	Jerome Bruner is born
1917	Urie Bronfenbrenner is born; Russian revolution takes place, with the Czar of Russia and his family being executed
1918	World War I ends and Spanish Flu breaks out, killing 50 to 100 million people
1920	Loris Malaguzzi born
1921	Reuven Feuerstein is born
1925	Albert Bandura is born
1929	Nel Noddings is born
1939	World War II breaks out
1943	Howard Gardner is born
1945	World War II ends
1952	Maria Montessori dies
1946	Loris Malaguzzi begins working as a teacher
1996	Te Whāriki commences

YouTube videos with additional insights into biographies and ideas of theorists

Locke	'John Locke's Thoughts on Education': www.youtube.com/watch?v=aaWjOqBAUPo
Rousseau	'Jean-Jacques Rousseau Biography (Cloud Biography)': www.youtube.com/watch?v=VqOaG24aPSc
Pestalozzi	'Johann Heinrich Pestalozzi Theory & Impact on Education Video & Lesson Transcript Education': www.youtube.com/watch?v=_fGbt2I3WBs
Froebel	'Froebel Kindergarten Gifts Early Childhood Education History of Toys': www.youtube.com/watch?v=LNBzmCKLNdU
McMillan	'Renaming the Education Building: Margaret McMillan': www.youtube.com/watch?v=BGG41ViX2H4
Montessori	'Maria Montessori': www.youtube.com/watch?v=TXqeTYHnOp4
Dewey	'John Dewey on Education': www.youtube.com/watch?v=P1mTlmTMgq8
Skinner	'The Early Life of B.F. Skinner': www.youtube.com/watch?v=Sf6oEPvHz58
Piaget	'Piaget on Piaget, Part 1': www.youtube.com/watch?v=I1JWr4G8YLM
Vygotsky	'Who was Vygotsky?': www.youtube.com/watch?v=bJTEUKYHyYo
Bandura	'Bandura's Social Cognitive Theory: An Introduction (Davidson Films, Inc.)': www.youtube.com/watch?v=S4N5J9jFW5U
Bronfenbrenner	'Urie Bronfenbrenner': www.youtube.com/watch?v=Au-7NHK3GGQ
Bruner	'Bruner's Constructivist Theory': www.youtube.com/watch?v=jm559ucUePg
Gardner	'Howard Gardner's Theory of Multiple Intelligences (Historical Overview)': www.youtube.com/watch?v=1wkFGXqJxas
Feuerstein	'Feuerstein Method': www.youtube.com/watch?v=oteFQ7x9ibk
Noddings	'Nel Noddings Care Theory': www.youtube.com/watch?v=SXbrQXPS1al

and crucial to later development. These initiatives also recognize that children's needs should be identified early on, especially in the case of children who might require additional support from such professionals as speech and language therapists, physiotherapists and educational psychologists. It has also been increasingly recognized by policy and decision makers that combining health assessments with education reviews in the early years can support professionals, parents and carers enormously in effective identification and intervention. A key factor underpinning all of these initiatives has been a growing acceptance that parents should be involved as much as possible and should be active participants where decisions are to be made about their children's learning and emotional development (MacBlain et al., 2017). Equally important has been the growing acceptance that children should, where possible, be part of any decision-making process and, crucially, be at the very centre of any review process.

FOREST SCHOOLS

Forest Schools, which have much of their origins in the work of practitioners at Bridgwater College, Somerset in the 1990s, have added a great deal to practice in the early years. The growth in Forest Schools and the principles that underpin this concept have, in the last two decades, been quite substantial with courses now being run for practitioners who wish to specialize in this area (see the following link, which offers a comprehensive overview of the nature of Forest Schools: www.forestschoolassociation.org/forest-school-myth-busting, accessed 31.07.17).

Early years practitioners have embraced opportunities for children's learning in the outdoors

---

ACTIVITIES AND POINTS FOR DISCUSSION

Activity: View the following website, The Nottinghamshire Children & Families Partnership: www.surestart.notts.nhs.uk – and identify the key factors that local authorities must take into account when supporting young children and their families.

Discussion Point: Consider why so many very young children growing up in the 21st century and their families still need high levels of support when this was recognized by theorists and philosophers such as Locke, Rousseau and Pestalozzi generations ago.

EXTENDED AND RECOMMENDED READING

Eisenstadt, N. (2011) *Providing a Sure Start: How Government Discovered Early Childhood*. Bristol: The Policy Press. (An informative and accessible account of the principles underpinning this important initiative.)

Lewis, J. (2011) 'From Sure Start to Children's Centres: an analysis of policy change in English early years programmes', *Journal of Social Policy*, 40(1): 71–88. (A very interesting and informative study.)

Mukherji, P. and Dryden, L. (eds) (2014) *Foundations of Early Childhood*. London: Sage.

National Children's Bureau (NCB), Early Childhood Unit (2015) *The Integrated Review: Bringing Together Health and Early Education Reviews at Age Two to Two-and-a-Half*. London: NCB. (An excellent insight into assessment at age 2 years and how different agencies work together.)

Office for Standards in Education, Children's Services and Skills (Ofsted) (2015) *The Report of Her Majesty's Chief Inspector of Education, Children's Services and Skills 2013–14 Social Care*. Manchester: Ofsted. (A thorough and informative study into the social aspects of children's development and learning.)

Additional information can be found on the following website relating to children's social development and learning, 'Early Years: The organisation for young children': www.early-years.org/surestart.

REFERENCES

De Botton, A. (2000) *The Consolations of Philosophy*. London: Hamish Hamilton.

Department for Education (DfE) (2012) *Statutory Framework for the Early Years Foundation Stage: Setting the Standards for Learning, Development and Care for Children from Birth to Five*. London: DfE. Contains public sector information licensed under the Open Government Licence v3.0: www.nationalarchives.gov.uk/doc/open-government-licence/version/3 (accessed 03.11.2017)

Department for Education (DfE) (2014) *Statutory Framework for the Early Years Foundation Stage: Setting the Standards for Learning, Development and Care for Children from Birth to Five*. London: DfE. Contains public sector information licensed under the Open Government Licence v2.0: www.nationalarchives.gov.uk/doc/open-government-licence/version/2 (accessed 03.11.2017)

Fitzgerald, D. and Kay, J. (2016) *Understanding Early Years Policy* (4th edn). London: Sage.

Jarvis, M. (2005) *The Psychology of Effective Learning and Teaching*. Cheltenham: Nelson Thornes.

MacBlain, S.F., Dunn, J. and Luke, I. (2017) *Contemporary Childhood*. London: Sage.

Miller, L. and Pound, L. (2011) *Theories and Approaches to Learning in the Early Years*. London: Sage.

National Children's Bureau (NCB), Early Childhood Unit (2015) *The Integrated Review: Bringing Together Health and Early Education Reviews at Age Two to Two-and-a-Half*. London: NCB.

Newby, P. (2010) *Research Methods for Education*. Harlow: Pearson Education.

Office for Standards in Education (Ofsted) (2006) *Extended Services in Schools and Children's Centres*. London: Ofsted.

Office for Standards in Education (Ofsted) (2008) *How Well are They Doing? The Impact of Children's Centres and Extended Schools*. London: Ofsted.

PART 1

EARLY INFLUENCES

Given the changing nature of the societies we live in, it is important to view the development of practice in early years education within a historical context. For this reason, it is necessary to understand how thinking has changed over generations and how the building blocks of what we now understand of children's early development have led to how practitioners think and work today. Clearly, theorists have viewed learning differently. This should not be viewed as problematic but, instead, should be seen as providing a richer and more eclectic means of understanding the complexities of children's learning. No two children are the same and each child learns differently, and the thinking that informs practice is so often a product of the historical time in which it evolves.

Each child brings to the learning process a unique set of intellectual skills and experiences

JOHN LOCKE AND THE EMERGENCE OF EMPIRICISM

THE THEORIST (1632–1704)

John Locke lived in a period when thinking was characterized largely by superstition, ignorance and religious intolerance, and yet he is considered to be one of our most enlightened thinkers. Locke was born in Somerset, England and lived through the beheading of King Charles, the English Civil Wars, Cromwell's Protectorate, the Restoration of King Charles II, the reigns of King James II and William and Mary, and the reign of Queen Anne. Locke also lived through the Great Plague of 1665–66 when around 15% of the population of London, in real figures – some 100,000 individuals, died. Such notable events must have impacted on how he viewed children's development and the purpose of education and learning.

KEY PUBLICATION

Locke, J. (1693) *Some Thoughts Concerning Education*. The Harvard Classics. New York: P.F. Collier & Son. Available at: www.bartleby.com/37/1 (accessed 06.11.17).

Children's earliest experiences all contribute to their learning

UNDERSTANDING THE THEORY

Amongst the many ideas offered by Locke was the notion that we should view children's minds as being like blank slates to be written on by their experiences of the world and the influences of others around them, or what has come to be known as *tabula rasa*.

TABULA RASA

Locke believed that children are born as blank slates or *tabula rasa* and it is upon these blank slates that their experiences are then written. Locke saw this process as being the very basis for children's learning. Importantly, Locke also believed that in addition to learning through experience, children need to learn how to apply reason when forming opinions and making interpretations of the world in which they live. Children, he argued, should be taught to question what is being told to them by those in authority. In proposing such a view, he was, in effect, reacting to much of the thinking of his time, which was so often steeped in superstition and fear; this was of course a time when many still believed the earth to be flat.

Locke saw the primary purpose of education as that of instilling within children the need for a strong sense of virtue. Unlike many of his contemporaries, he felt that learning should be enjoyable and that children's experience of learning could be positively enhanced through encouragement from adults who could and should also provide guidance in helping children learn how to learn. In this final respect, he was years ahead of his time and, like many theorists who came generations later, Locke recognized and expounded the importance of language as being central to children's learning.

EMPIRICISM

Locke can be described as belonging to that group of thinkers known as the *empiricists*. Central to their philosophy of learning was the notion of 'empirical thinking', which is at the very heart of the sciences where phenomena are observed, and information in the form of data is gathered and quantified and then objectively analysed. *Empiricism* proposes that children's learning, which results from external experiences gained through sensory stimuli, is best understood through systematic and planned observation and subsequent analysis of their behaviours. *Empiricism* differs from *nativism*, which holds that children inherit abilities. *Empiricism* grew substantially between World War I and World War II and was embraced by those working in the field of psychology, most especially the *behaviourists*. In effect, *empiricism* offered psychology a methodology, at the heart of which lay the observation, recording and measurement of behaviours (Gross, 1992; Smith et al., 2003). This then led to explorations of learning by psychologists wishing to apply the objective principles that *empiricism* offered.

WHAT THE THEORY LOOKS LIKE IN PRACTICE

Though Locke lived some centuries ago, it is, nevertheless, possible to observe on a daily basis some of the ideas that were central to his original

The power of reasoning can be observed in activities that present a challenge

philosophy of learning. Locke believed, for example, that play was an essential part of children's development and argued strongly that adults should take care not to hinder children in their play, nor from 'being children'. Unlike in previous generations where children were forced into employment at an early age, often having to work in dreadful conditions, children are now encouraged and supported in 'being children' and absorbing themselves in their play. Locke also believed that children should not only have healthy minds but also healthy bodies and he believed strongly in the power of reasoning; it is possible to observe teachers and practitioners in schools and early years settings developing children's critical reasoning skills and abilities.

Locke also believed that learning should not be a burden, nor should it be imposed on children with tasks that might become 'irksome' and inhibit their learning. Within early years settings and primary schools, we view teachers and practitioners taking care to ensure that the activities that children engage in are creative, carefully managed to promote motivation and directed in such a way that children's learning is cumulative and purposeful, whilst also being enjoyable and motivating. Locke believed strongly that children should not be pressured into having to deal with aspects of learning that are 'serious' for 'their minds, nor bodies will bear it. It injures their health'. He viewed such pressures placed on young children as being responsible for why 'a great many have hated books and learning all their lives'. Early years practitioners now take great care to ensure that children are not placed under too much pressure.

STRENGTHS AND WEAKNESSES OF THE THEORY

It can be said with confidence that Locke set out many of the basic foundations upon which our current understanding of learning has been built. Indeed, others, such as Pestalozzi, Froebel, Dewey and Montessori, who followed Locke shared much of his thinking. A major strength of Locke's work is his contribution to empirical thinking, which lies at the very heart of psychology and provided the *behaviourists* with a clear methodology. Perhaps the only weakness of Locke's theoretical perspective is that it was created at a time when society was so very different to today. That said, many of the characteristics that defined the society of Locke's time can still be seen today, if one looks hard enough.

CASE STUDY: ALLOWING CHILDREN TO BE CHILDREN

The following example, taken from MacBlain and Bowman (2016, p. 75), clearly indicates the length to which practitioners in one particular early years setting have gone to ensure that play is not overly directed by adults, is creative and motivational and places the child at the very centre of the activity:

> Children are encouraged to make informed choices about their play ... The curriculum is carefully planned and organized with the children's interests being central to all that the staff do. Activities are revisited in order to give the children that important time and cognitive-temporal space in which they can develop new skills and, importantly, establish consolidations and connections within their learning.

CASE STUDY: THE IMPORTANCE OF REASONING

Harry's teacher is keen to promote critical thinking skills in her playgroup and devotes some time each week to engaging the children in activities that will encourage them to think more objectively and more critically. She introduces new tasks that require the children to solve problems, work in groups and reach decisions. The tasks challenge the children to think about sensitive issues such as helping a child who is upset and how they should listen to the points of views expressed by other children. As the weeks unfold, Harry's teacher notes how the children listen more carefully to one another, give each other time to express ideas and conclusions and hold back from rushing to express their own views. The children appear to give more time to reasoning and less to simply reacting at an emotional level when they disagree with others in their groups.

LINKS TO OTHER THEORIES

Like many theorists that followed him, such as Rousseau, Pestalozzi and Froebel, Locke believed strongly that childhood is a time when children should enjoy learning. Like the behaviourists who came generations later, he suggested that elements of children's learning could be systematically observed, measured and quantified in an objective way.

ACTIVITIES AND POINTS FOR DISCUSSION

Activity: Identify the key points that are central to Locke's philosophy and how these have influenced thinking and practice in early years education over previous generations.

Discussion Point: Consider why Locke's ideas were taken up by some practitioners over previous generations but were not taken up by others. Why might some practitioners and teachers have resisted his ideas?

EXTENDED AND RECOMMENDED READING

Gray, C. and MacBlain, S.F. (2015) *Learning Theories in Childhood* (2nd edn). London: Sage.

REFERENCES

Gross, R. (1992) *Psychology: The Science of Mind and Behaviour*. London: Hodder & Stoughton.

MacBlain, S.F. and Bowman, H. (2016) 'Teaching and learning', in D. Wyse and S. Rogers (eds), *A Guide to Early Years and Primary Teaching* (pp. 66–84). London: Sage.

Smith, K.S., Cowie, H. and Blades, M. (2003) *Understanding Children's Development* (4th edn). Oxford: Blackwell.

JEAN-JACQUES ROUSSEAU AND THE CONCEPT OF 'CHILD'

THE THEORIST (1712–1778)

Rousseau's ideas came at a time when childhood was poorly understood and children were often viewed as 'little adults' and put to work from an early age. Many children, at the time, failed to have any real experience of play, instead growing up with expectations that they would be put to manual labour and have little if any education. The education of girls was vastly different to that of boys, with daughters of more affluent parents being reared largely for marriage into 'good' families and those from poorer parents for the world of work and drudgery. An interesting feature of Rousseau's own life as a parent was that he sent his children off to an orphanage.

KEY PUBLICATION

Rousseau, J.J. (1911) *Emile*. London: J.M. Dent.

Love and security in early childhood are the very basis of future learning

UNDERSTANDING THE THEORY

Much of the thinking around childhood in Rousseau's time centred on the notion of 'original sin', with a key function of education being a desire to purge children of this sin and the associated guilt that went with it. It was popularly believed, for example, that children were born with internal drives, needs and impulses, which, if not addressed, could lead to 'wickedness' (MacBlain, 2014). Rousseau, by contrast, believed that children were born good and inherited much of what would make up their individual abilities, characters and potential. He knew, however, that the societies children were born into played a crucial role in influencing their development and recognized the potential harm societies could create in perverting the thinking and behaviour of children.

The education experienced by many young children at the time was often severe and almost universally adult-led, and, for most children, formal learning was an unhappy experience to be endured and even suffered, rather than being enjoyed. Little consideration was given to children's feelings and emotions or to their happiness and it was common practice for parents to place their newly born infants with wet nurses. Rousseau challenged this type of thinking and in doing so radically changed the beliefs held by many parents. He was, for example, a great proponent of breastfeeding and emphasized the importance of newly born infants bonding emotionally with their mothers. More particularly, he applied great effort to emphasizing the need for children to not only experience freedom during childhood as a means of developing their learning; he was also a strong advocate of the idea that childhood should be a time of happiness.

BEING A CHILD: THE ART OF FORMING MEN

Rousseau saw the primary function of education as that of '*l'art de former des hommes*' (the art of forming men) and viewed education as a mechanism through which children would come to benefit the societies in which they lived, in addition to receiving information and knowledge. Rousseau set out his ideas on educating children in his celebrated book *Emile* (1911) in which he introduced readers to the life of a young boy named Emile as he progressed from infancy to adulthood. Rousseau saw children as passing through stages and in doing so recognized how learning is developmental. For Rousseau, the first stage that children go through is from birth to 12 when children are predominantly influenced by impulses and by their emotions. The second stage is up to the age of 16 when, Rousseau believed, reason takes over and begins to replace actions led by emotions and impulses. Following this second stage, the young person then moves into adulthood. It should be recognized that Rousseau's emphasis on this innate development of human nature formed the philosophical basis for the views of later thinkers and practitioners and, perhaps most notably, those of Pestalozzi.

THE ROLE OF THE TUTOR

Rousseau saw the primary role of the teacher to be one of channelling those drives, needs and impulses that children are born with, in a positive and purposeful way that would then come to benefit society as a whole. He believed that children's education should, as far as possible, follow children's natural growth. This would be in contrast to the demands made on them by the societies and cultures in which they lived. Indeed, he further viewed the role of the teacher as central to creating and managing learning environments that would be positive and effective and where children could be introduced to new and purposeful learning. It was through such a process that children could, he argued, come to properly understand the world in which they lived and internalize a better understanding of themselves and others. This process would also, he believed, guide children in understanding the difference between right and wrong and the consequences of their actions, in addition to learning humility and having empathy for others.

WHAT THE THEORY LOOKS LIKE IN PRACTICE

Whilst Rousseau's ideas were developed generations ago, it is still possible to recognize the principles behind his ideas and theory in many early years settings. Take the following two case studies.

Freedom is one of the building blocks of early learning

We begin understanding the world through our first experiences of observing adults

CASE STUDY: FREEDOM TO THINK AND LEARN

Martha has just started working at a local nursery and is talking with one of the parents who is expressing concerns about the children 'playing far too much'. She feels that the children spend 'far too much time playing' and should be 'learning to read and write and do basic maths'. Martha begins to explain to the parent that play is a very important part of learning and that through play children develop their thinking by constructing new understanding through trying things out, collaborating with others and developing their language and physical skills and abilities. The parent accepts what Martha is saying and tells her that she had 'never thought about play like that before'.

Creating their own learning environments encourages children to think differently

CASE STUDY: TAKING TIME TO OBSERVE CHILDREN'S NATURAL LEARNING

Tania is on her first placement as a student at a local nursery and is shadowing her mentor outside whilst the children involve themselves in play activities. She takes time to focus on one particular child who appears absorbed in picking up dandelions, which have turned to seed. The child blows the top of the dandelion and watches as the little white seeds are carried away with her blowing. Tania begins to consider the child's activity as more than just blowing and occupying herself and, instead, begins to reflect on how the child is engaging with nature and through this engagement is starting a learning process whereby she begins to understand that plants, such as the dandelion, can change shape and structure and can begin to seed themselves. Tania walks to the child and tells her how her blowing is like the wind and that when the wind blows it is helping to disperse the seeds from the dandelion so that more dandelions will grow elsewhere.

STRENGTHS AND WEAKNESSES OF THE THEORY

A major strength of Rousseau's theory is that it has endured over the centuries. Rousseau was enlightened in his thinking and introduced many to the notion that children are born with the potential to become active and empathetic members of society. He was ahead of his time in asserting that the role of the teacher is crucial in not only supporting children's learning but also in supporting their social and emotional development. His ideas have, however, been criticized on the grounds that he was too open to the notion that the impulses children are born with are their true impulses. It must be emphasized that his ideas were in many respects compromised by the world he was born into. Rousseau's ideas on education have also been open to criticism on the grounds that they related to boys; girls at the time were expected to demonstrate obedience.

LINKS TO OTHER THEORIES

Like other theorists and philosophers that followed him, Rousseau placed great emphasis on the child being at the centre of the learning process. Later theorists drew on many of his ideas, developing these further and embedding them within practice. Like

Piaget, Rousseau saw children as passing through developmental stages and, like Bronfenbrenner who succeeded him some generations later, he emphasized the importance of understanding children's learning and development within wider economic, social and political contexts.

Children need to be at the very centre of their learning experiences

ACTIVITIES AND POINTS FOR DISCUSSION

Activity: Identify a number of factors that characterized the society in which Rousseau lived and that might have impacted negatively on young children, and then consider if similar factors continue to exist today.

Discussion Point: What steps can early years practitioners take to develop within children a strong sense of belonging to a community?

EXTENDED AND RECOMMENDED READING

Access the following link to the Rousseau association: www.rousseauassociation.org, which offers a wealth of additional material and information on Rousseau's ideas.

REFERENCES

MacBlain, S.F. (2014) *How Children Learn*. London: Sage.

Rousseau, J.J. (1911) *Emile*. London: J.M. Dent.

JOHANN PESTALOZZI AND THE IMPORTANCE OF NATURE

THE THEORIST (1746–1827)

Johann Pestalozzi was born in Zurich, Switzerland. His father died when he was only 5 years of age and for much of his life he lived in poverty. This deeply affected Johann, though it also provided him with the means to empathize with children from very poor families and to understand, at first hand, how they were affected by poverty. Pestalozzi was heavily influenced by Rousseau and opened a school in 1805. He is often referred to as the father of modern education.

KEY PUBLICATION

Pestalozzi, J.H. (1894) *How Gertrude Teaches Her Children* (trans. L.E. Holland and F.C. Turner; edited with an introduction by E. Cooke). London: Swan Sonnenschein.

Nature forms a unique and wonderful source of learning for all children

UNDERSTANDING THE THEORY

Pestalozzi (1894) believed that all children should be entitled to an education; he viewed much of the education on offer at the time to children as irrelevant and of little real use to children from poor families. He believed that a primary aim of education was to develop the *head*, the *heart* and the *hands*, and he proposed that attention to these three aspects would create children who knew right from wrong and who could behave as individuals in ways that were informed by knowledge; the result, he suggested, would be a happier society. His ideas were well expressed by Silber (1965, p. 134) some decades ago, who quoted him as follows:

I wish to wrest education from the outworn order of doddering old teaching hacks as well as from the new-fangled order of cheap, artificial teaching tricks, and entrust it to the eternal powers of nature herself, to the light which God has kindled and kept alive in the hearts of fathers and mothers, to the

interests of parents who desire their children grow up in favour with God and with men.

In many respects, his ideas on education and learning were ahead of their time. Pestalozzi believed strongly, for example, that children should learn through actively engaging in activities and through using many of the objects they came into contact with in their environments. Importantly, he also believed that children should be free to follow their own interests and could learn effectively by doing so.

THE FATHER OF PEDAGOGY

Pestalozzi believed that teaching was a subject that should be studied in its own right and because of this he is often seen as the father of pedagogy. Indeed, his contributions to our understanding of children's learning led to education being viewed as a distinct form of knowledge to be explored and researched, which has been very much the case in recent decades with students, for example, taking professional training programmes at university.

ACTIVITY AND SPONTANEITY

Pestalozzi saw spontaneity as a key feature of children's learning and was a strong advocate of the view that children should not be limited to receiving 'set' answers from adults to their questions but, instead, should be encouraged to explore their own thinking and to gain further knowledge through activity. In this way, he argued, children could cultivate higher order thinking such as reasoning and, in this respect, he saw the role of education as being that of educating the 'whole child' and felt that education should be in line with nature.

Being encouraged to explore their own thinking is central to children's intellectual development

THE IMPORTANCE OF THE HOME

Pestalozzi emphasized the importance of the home as a place where children should be cared for and nurtured. He believed strongly that the home was where children could and should find happiness and that the home formed the basis for all future learning. He saw much of the education of his time as uninteresting, irrelevant and too adult-led.

WHAT THE THEORY LOOKS LIKE IN PRACTICE

Whilst Pestalozzi formed his ideas some hundreds of years ago, there are many aspects of his theory that remain relevant even today. Practitioners working with children in early years settings, for example, take great care to structure activities and new learning in such a way that they address the 'whole' child. They also take care to support positive social and emotional development of their children and can be observed doing this by, for example, taking time to listen to children, observing them in their attempts to collaborate with their peers and guiding them sensitively with this and with building relationships. They place great emphasis on ensuring that the children they work with are happy and experience learning in a way that supports their well-being, recognize the importance of children's experiences in their homes and typically work in purposeful ways to ensure that parents of the children feel supported.

STRENGTHS AND WEAKNESSES OF THE THEORY

Like most theories that have been formed generations ago, it is difficult to say with certainty what weaknesses there are, if any, as the theorists were working and writing at a time in history that was so vastly different to today. Pestalozzi's theory is, however, one that offers a great many strengths, which have sustained thinking and practice over the generations. He is still viewed, for example, as the 'father' of pedagogy and set out a vision that, even today, influences how we think about children's learning and development.

LINKS TO OTHER THEORIES

Pestalozzi was influenced by the ideas of Locke and Rousseau, and, like other theorists who came later,

CASE STUDY: SUPPORTING CHILDREN'S LEARNING THROUGH PARTNERSHIP

Jessica is 3 years old and lives with her mother who is a lone parent. Jessica's mother has been unemployed for a number of years and struggles to make ends meet. She found that when Jessica started at the nursery the staff were extremely supportive and took time to talk with her several times a week at the end of the day. Jessica's mother feels that Jessica is very happy at the nursery and because of this she feels that this is an area of her life that she does not have to be anxious about, as Jessica always gets excited when going to the nursery in the morning and at the end of the day. Jessica's mother also feels that she can talk to any of the staff at the nursery and almost sees them as friends.

CASE STUDY: LEARNING BY DOING

Abby has just started working at a local playgroup, which is in an economically deprived inner-city area, characterized by low incomes and poverty. Abby has just completed her training in early years and has been influenced by the writings and ideas of Pestalozzi who was the focus of her final year project. She is determined to link the *head* with the *heart* and the *hands* of the children she is going to work with. She determines to engage the children in learning that is characterized by doing, sharing and collaborating with peers and being sensitive to others' needs. At the end of her first term, she is congratulated by her manager who draws attention to how the children engage in activities with purpose and excitement, how they share with one another and the improvements in their emotional well-being.

he saw the importance of children living happy, free and meaningful lives. Much of his thinking served to influence later theorists such as Montessori and Steiner, and it can be argued with confidence that his ideas on education and the importance of learning through nature can be seen throughout the theories of many others and well into the 20th century with their influence on Forest School. A key link to Pestalozzi's theory can be found in the ideas of Nel Noddings, later in this text, who placed great emphasis on the relationship between 'care' in the early years and learning.

ACTIVITIES AND POINTS FOR DISCUSSION

Activity: Identify examples of children's learning that have involved spontaneity on their part. What was it about the situation that encouraged and facilitated their spontaneity?

Discussion Point: Are children today given enough opportunities in their learning to develop their spontaneity and if not, why not?

EXTENDED AND RECOMMENDED READING

Fitzgerald, D. and Kay, J. (2016) *Understanding Early Years Policy* (4th edn). London: Sage. (An excellent overview of early years policy and practice in the UK that can be used as a means of making comparisons between current practice and that of Pestalozzi and other early theorists.)

Gray, C. and MacBlain, S.F. (2015) *Learning Theories in Childhood* (2nd edn). London: Sage.

Reed, M. and Walker, R. (eds) (2014) *A Critical Companion to Early Childhood*. London: Sage. (A critical and informative text that looks at a range of topics in early years practice, such as professionalism and the curriculum.)

REFERENCES

Pestalozzi, J.H. (1894) *How Gertrude Teaches Her Children* (trans. L.E. Holland and F.C. Turner; edited with an introduction by E. Cooke). London: Swan Sonnenschein.

Silber, K. (1965) *Pestalozzi: The Man and His Work*. London: Routledge & Kegan Paul.

FRIEDRICH FROEBEL AND THE IMPORTANCE OF PLAY

THE THEORIST (1782–1852)

Friedrich Froebel was born in 1782 in Oberweißach in what is now Germany. He was an impulsive young man and held a number of different jobs before taking up a position as teacher in a school in Frankfurt under the direction of Anton Gruner, who had opened a school following the progressive principles originally established by the Swiss educator and reformer Johann Pestalozzi. Whilst working at this school, Froebel realized his desire to be a teacher, opening his own school in 1816. Ten years later, he published *On the Education of Man*, which set out his own philosophy of education and the methods he would implement within his own school. Some years later, in 1831, the Swiss government invited Froebel to become involved in training teachers who wished to work with young children. In 1837, he established a school for young children, which he named 'kindergarten'.

KEY PUBLICATION

Froebel, F. (1887) *The Education of Man*. New York: D. Appleton Century.

UNDERSTANDING THE THEORY

Froebel (1887) was one of the first theorists to fully acknowledge the value of play and its importance for children's learning and social and emotional development. Indeed, Froebel's ideas on learning in early childhood continue to influence practice even today. His theory has also had a huge influence on how we have come to view the nature of learning in young children and especially how play can support and extend new learning. Froebel saw the value of children expressing themselves through play, which lay at the core of his thinking. The importance of his ideas on play and how it supports learning was demonstrated some years ago by Tizard and Hughes

(1984, p. 4) who emphasized how the kindergarten and nursery school started by Froebel 'freed' young children from the type of education of the day when most children sat passively each day being drilled by their teachers and subjected to enormous amounts of rote learning.

Froebel developed a range of educational materials that could facilitate learning in young children (Gray and MacBlain, 2015). These materials or 'gifts', as Froebel referred to them, included such things as differently shaped objects, like squared blocks and spheres, that could be used for stimulating thinking and learning, for example:

> Gift 1: Six small soft balls, possibly knitted or made of rubber, three of which are in primary colours, red, yellow and blue, and three in secondary colours, green, orange and purple.

> Gift 2: A box containing a wooden cylinder, a cube and a sphere containing holes.

> Gift 3: A box containing eight one-inch wooden cubes.

> Gift 4: New shapes of different sizes and dimensions.

> Gift 5: A box of a different size from those above, as are the blocks within the box, which have increased in number.

Froebel believed strongly in the importance of children being active and learning through engaging in tasks that are purposeful and have meaning for the children. It must be emphasized, of course, that at the time he was proposing these ideas, childhood was poorly understood. A popular perception of childhood at the time was to view children as little adults; indeed, children were often considered to be adults on reaching the age of 7. Even very young children were sent to work and few had any access to education, particularly girls, with many children growing up illiterate. In emphasizing the importance of children engaging actively in tasks that are purposeful and have meaning as being key to their learning, Froebel developed what have been referred to as 'occupations'. He also emphasized the

Shapes and objects in the environment provide a natural source for supporting learning

importance of children being active out of doors and learning from and through nature; and he introduced us to the notion of the 'kindergarten'. Froebel viewed the environment in which children learn as being extremely important, and he believed strongly in the potential that music might have in children's learning and especially the value of singing whilst involved in play.

WHAT THE THEORY LOOKS LIKE IN PRACTICE

It is possible to observe many aspects of Froebel's original ideas even today. Early years practitioners, for example, place great emphasis on the importance of play and how it impacts positively on learning and social and emotional development. Children in early years settings can be observed using materials such as blocks, shapes and patterns to develop their learning. They use blocks to build and to count and to extend their gross and fine motor coordination. Play is viewed as immensely valuable, with a clear purpose that underpins important language development.

STRENGTHS AND WEAKNESSES OF THE THEORY

It is safe to suggest that the strengths of Froebel's theory significantly outweigh any weaknesses. His ideas were, in many respects, generations ahead of his time and continue to influence thinking and practice today. His thoughts and ideas about the importance of play and how practitioners can add structure to learning activities and situations without being intrusive or controlling, are most enlightening. Miller and Pound (2011, p. 64) have commented on how those who promoted Froebel's ideas in previous decades have exerted an influence on official policy, 'from the Hadow report (1933) onwards … to The Early Years Foundation Stage (CCSF, 2008)'. They have also commented on a more recent trend in Froebel training: 'the next generation of Froebelians is emerging, trained in the practical apprenticeship way, in reflective practice through in-service training'.

LINKS TO OTHER THEORIES

Froebel was influenced by the ideas of Pestalozzi and particularly Pestalozzi's emphasis on learning through activity. He was also greatly influenced by the ideas set out by Rousseau in regard to children developing holistically and contributing positively to the societies

CASE STUDY: THE 'GIFTS' – USING BLOCKS TO PROVIDE STRUCTURE IN LEARNING

Diane has just commenced her placement at a local nursery school and has been asked to work with a group of four 3-year-old children after their morning break. On her first day at the nursery, she identified lots of wooden blocks of different shapes and sizes. She decides that she will collect these and place them on the carpet in a corner of the room and then invite the children to play with them. She calculates that around half an hour will be adequate time. She presents the activity as one where the children have to remove the wooden blocks carefully from a large box and then work together to build one particular structure rather than knocking down individual ones and starting again. She also listens intently to their conversations and hears them extending their language by copying each other's words and phrases. She further notes that they are developing their skills in collaborating with one another, as well as developing their fine motor skills and coordination, as they carefully build one block upon another and choose shapes that fit with one another and suit the structures they are building.

CASE STUDY: SUPPORTING LEARNING THROUGH EXPERIENCE

Alex attends a local nursery, where practice has been inspired by many of Froebel's original ideas. As part of the curriculum, the nursery includes a wide range of musical activities. Most days, Alex is encouraged to take part in musical activities that include rhyme, rhythm with clapping and general movement. Along with the other children, Alex is also supported by the adults in making his own musical instruments using materials such as cardboard and paper, and to compose new songs. Alex greatly enjoys these sessions. On occasions, Alex sits in a circle with the other children and adults and they sing songs together whilst clapping their hands to the rhythm.

Through play children can externalize their inner thinking and creativity

in which they grow up. It is important to understand that Froebel's ideas, though conceived generations ago, have continued to remain at the heart of more recent theorists' thinking, many of whom have placed great value on the importance of play, creativity and children learning through actively engaging in purposeful and meaningful tasks. These are ideas common to more contemporary theorists, such as Dewey, Piaget, Bruner, Bandura, Vygotsky and Noddings.

ACTIVITIES AND POINTS FOR DISCUSSION

Activity: View this link on the internet to 'Yellow Dot Nursery': www.yellowdotnursery.co.uk/Friedrich_Froebel.cfm, and identify those aspects of the curriculum that are underpinned by Froebel's ideas.

Discussion Point: Discuss how relevant Froebel's ideas are today for children with special educational needs and/or disabilities.

EXTENDED AND RECOMMENDED READING

Campbell-Barr, V. and Leeson, C. (2016) *Quality and Leadership in the Early Years: Theory and Practice*. London: Sage. (An accessible and informative text that examines policy and practice in the early years and how these are influenced by leadership.)

Much additional information can be found at the website: http://froebeltoday.com

REFERENCES

Froebel, F. (1887) *The Education of Man*. New York: D. Appleton Century.

Gray, C. and MacBlain, S.F. (2015) *Learning Theories in Childhood* (2nd edn). London: Sage.

Miller, L. and Pound, L. (2011) *Theories and Approaches to Learning in the Early Years*. London: Sage.

Tizard, B. and Hughes, M. (1984) *Young Children Learning: Learning and Thinking at Home and at School*. London: Fontana.

RACHEL AND MARGARET MCMILLAN AND SOCIAL REFORM

THE THEORIST (RACHEL, 1859–1917; MARGARET, 1860–1931)

Rachel and Margaret's parents emigrated in 1840 from Scotland to America and in 1865 they sadly lost their father, James, along with their younger sister, Elizabeth. Margaret was just 5 years of age at the time. Their mother then returned to Scotland with Rachel and Margaret and in 1877 she also died. Rachel later moved to London in 1888 to be closer to her sister. In subsequent years, Margaret played an influential role in the training of teachers and founded the *Rachel McMillan College* in 1930 for training teachers and improving the training of those working with children in her nurseries.

KEY PUBLICATIONS

McMillan, M. (1904) *Education through the Imagination*. London: J.M. Dent. (Available at the following link: https://archive.org/details/educationthroug01mcmigoog, accessed 31.07.17).

McMillan, M. (1919) *The Nursery School*. London: J.M. Dent & Sons. [revised 1930]

Access to the outdoors provides numerous opportunities for active learning and collaboration

UNDERSTANDING THE THEORY

To fully understand the contributions made by Rachel and Margaret McMillan, we need to first understand the society they lived in. All major cities in England were, at the time, characterized by extremes of wealth and poverty, with attempts being made, sometimes more successfully than others, by visionary individuals and charitable organizations at introducing social reform. London, for example, offered some of the worst living conditions in Europe, with a distinct lack of sanitation, some of the highest mortality rates in childhood and a place amongst the worst slums. In the three decades between 1831 and 1866, some 150,000 children and adults died from cholera. Indeed, Londoners living in the 1840s might expect to live for only 30–40 years. By 1911 this had improved and people could expect to live, on average, into their fifties (Hall, 1998). Horn (1997) has estimated that between 1900 and 1950 around 30,000 homeless children lived on the streets of London. The age of consent in the mid-1800s was 12 years of age, with many children being unsupervised and growing up with little or no education.

It was only in 1899, ten years after the first murders of the infamous Jack the Ripper took place in London, that attendance at school became compulsory; this was the London that Rachel moved to, in order to be with her sister, Margaret. After much effort, the sisters succeeded in their quest for children to have free school meals, following the enactment of the Provision of School Meals Act in 1906. The sisters were also influential in the government, introducing medical inspections of children in schools, with the first clinic opening in 1908. Rachel and Margaret were especially outspoken in their insistence that the first years of children's lives were of crucial importance. True to their belief, they founded what has come to be known as the *Nursery Movement*. They also saw the benefits of open-air learning, which was a reaction to the overcrowded and filthy living conditions in which thousands of children lived and grew up. Like Margaret, Rachel believed that involving children in nurseries in the care of animals and plants was a means of developing within them the important values of caring not only for themselves but also for others.

Caring for animals and plants is a means of learning to care not only for ourselves but also for others

deprived areas, where children often have less access to nature and the countryside than their suburban and rural counterparts.

WHAT THE THEORY LOOKS LIKE IN PRACTICE

Rachel and Margaret McMillan placed enormous emphasis on the importance of children being healthy and having access to the outdoors. One can observe in most, if not all, early years settings today, children having access to the outdoors through, for example, Forest School, the clear emphasis given to outdoors play and the promotion by practitioners of children having a balanced and nutritious diet. This emphasis can be found especially in inner-city and socially

STRENGTHS AND WEAKNESSES OF THE THEORY

Rachel and Margaret McMillan have offered early years practitioners a wonderful legacy, which has at its core the importance of children's health and well-being. Readers may wish to consider how their thinking impacted so significantly on the lives of countless children at a time when poverty was rife and little was made of the links between poor diet, poverty and learning. Readers may also wish to consider how relevant their ideas are today as significant numbers of children in the UK are growing up in an era of heightened austerity and marked poverty. The number of children in the UK, for example, who are growing up in households that now rely on food banks has been increasing over the last few years.

CASE STUDY: LEARNING THE VALUE OF CARING

Ben is 5 years of age and has just started at his local school. On his first day, Ben's teacher takes his whole class outside to a small fenced off area behind the school building where she keeps a number of pets. It is called the *Pet Den*. Ben's teacher introduces the children to each of the pets in turn and then demonstrates how to feed them. On the following day, Ben and his classmates are given the opportunity to feed each pet in turn just as the teacher has done. Over the coming weeks, they are given responsibility for checking the pets and feeding them.

CASE STUDY: THE IMPORTANCE OF THE OUTDOORS

Azmeena and Pradeep have grown up and currently live in the centre of a large city where they attend a local playgroup, which places a great deal of emphasis on learning outside. Whenever the weather looks fine, the children are encouraged to play out and to engage in learning activities outside where they can enjoy the fresh air and experience the sensations of warmth, wind and even cold, and sometimes rain and occasionally snow. Staff at the playgroup believe that learning outside adds much to the experience of their children, many of whom tend to sit indoors when at home and to have few opportunities to play out. The staff have observed how playing and engaging in activities outside promotes better concentration, offers new opportunities to work collaboratively and motivates the children to attempt new and challenging tasks.

LINKS TO OTHER THEORIES

Like Rousseau, Pestalozzi and Froebel, the McMillan sisters stressed the importance of seeing young children as individuals and as being at a stage in their lives where they are vulnerable and in need of care, love and support from adults. Like other theorists, they challenged the thinking of their time and, like later theorists such as Dewey and Steiner, initiated new ways of structuring children's learning environments, placing specific emphasis on the importance of nature and the outdoors.

ACTIVITIES AND POINTS FOR DISCUSSION

Activity: List the benefits that visits to local parks, recreation grounds and woodlands can have for very young children who live in inner-city areas.

Discussion Point: What can adults in early years settings do to support children in developing good health?

EXTENDED AND RECOMMENDED READING

Dahlberg, G., Moss, P. and Pence, A. (2013) *Beyond Quality in Early Childhood Education and Care: Languages of Evaluation*. London: Routledge. (A comprehensive text focusing on quality in early years practice.)

Gray, C. and MacBlain, S.F. (2015) *Learning Theories in Childhood* (2nd edn). London: Sage.

REFERENCES

Hall, P. (1998) *Cities in Civilisation*. London: Weidenfeld & Nicolson.

Horn, P. (1997) *The Victorian Town Child*. Stroud: Sutton.

SIGMUND FREUD AND THE PSYCHODYNAMIC TRADITION

THE THEORIST (1856–1939)

Freud was born in Freiberg, Moravia and at 4 years of age moved with his family to Vienna in Austria where he lived and worked throughout his life. In 1938 the Nazis annexed Austria and Freud, who was Jewish, was permitted to leave for England. Freud originally qualified as a doctor though he also studied philosophy and physiology. He is often associated with the practice of hypnosis, which he used in the early stages of practising psychoanalysis. Freud was more interested in working with adults than children, unlike his daughter Anna Freud who followed her father into practising psychoanalysis, preferring to focus on working with children.

KEY PUBLICATIONS

Freud, S. (1900) *The Interpretation of Dreams*. SE, 4–5.

Freud, S. (1915) *The Unconscious*. SE, 14: 159–204.

Freud, S. (1920) *Beyond the Pleasure Principle*. SE, 18: 1–64.

Freud, S. (1923) *The Ego and the Id*. SE, 19: 1–66.

SE, *The Standard Edition of the Complete Psychological Works of Sigmund Freud* (ed. J. Strachey et al.), 24 Vols. London: Hogarth Press, 1956–1974.

UNDERSTANDING THE THEORY

Freud is considered a key figure in the emergence of psychology and is most closely associated with the field of *psychodynamics*, particularly *psychoanalysis*. Though controversial, Freud's contribution to our understanding of childhood has, nevertheless, been substantial (MacBlain, 2014). Miller and Pound (2011, p. 22) have, for example, emphasized how the legacy of ideas offered by psychoanalysts have become 'embedded in the culture of the industrially

Loving relationships formed in the first years provide security and stability for later learning

developed world, including in relation to the development and care of children'.

IDIOGRAPHIC AND NOMOTHETIC APPROACHES

It is helpful when seeking to understand the psychodynamic tradition and its contribution to our understanding of children's development and learning to consider two quite different approaches, namely the *idiographic* and the *nomothetic*. The first of these views individuals as being wholly unique; any study of children, therefore, must begin with this premise. The nomothetic approach, on the other hand, seeks to identify patterns in human behaviours, often referred to as traits, and asserts that through studying these patterns or traits it is possible to understand the development of individuals. In essence, the work of Freud and subsequent psychodynamic theorists lies within the idiographic approach.

Freud proposed that at the heart of individual development lie two determining elements, characterized by pleasure and by tensions. He suggested that tensions in individuals arise from sexual energy (the libido) and that pleasure in individuals emanates from a release of this sexual energy. It should be noted that Freud employed the term 'sexual' in quite a broad way, to account for all those thoughts and actions that individuals find pleasurable. In developing his theory, Freud took the view that individuals move through a series of stages, with the first of these being the oral stage (McLeod, 2008).

ORAL STAGE (BIRTH TO AROUND 12 MONTHS)

At this stage, children's personality is being shaped by their libido, which centres on the mouth. Children derive satisfaction through putting most things in their mouths, which in a sense meets the needs of their libido. One can observe very young children putting all manner of objects in their mouths; they also suck objects in addition to breastfeeding or being fed with a bottle. Freud suggested that over-stimulation at this stage can result in children developing oral fixations later on in their lives, which might be manifested by such behaviours as smoking and thumb sucking, which he suggested may become accentuated when individuals experience stress in their lives.

ANAL STAGE (12 MONTHS TO AROUND 36 MONTHS)

Freud suggested that, at this stage, children's libido has become more concentrated on the anus, with children experiencing pleasure when defecating. Freud believed that as children move into this stage they have already started to view themselves as individuals. A process of realization has commenced whereby children are becoming increasingly aware that their own needs, wishes and desires can conflict with those of others. Excessive conflict encountered at this stage or having overly severe boundaries imposed on them by adults may, Freud suggested, govern how children relate to authority when older, even having an overly exaggerated and unnecessary respect for authority. Insisting, for example, that children engage with potty training at too early a stage can, Freud suggested, result in children growing into adults who are anally retentive, with behaviour patterns characterized by

a need to be excessively clean and tidy. Freud suggested that conflicts during the anal stage can also result in children becoming overly stubborn and miserly when they are adults.

PHALLIC STAGE (36 MONTHS TO AROUND 5/6 YEARS OF AGE)

By this stage, children's personality development is becoming centred around their genitals, with masturbation offering a new sense of pleasure. Children are now becoming increasingly aware of the differences between the sexes. Freud believed that this developing awareness brings with it degrees of conflict typically manifested by physical attraction to others but also by rivalry and even jealousy and fear. He referred to this process as the *Oedipus complex* in boys and, in girls, the *Electra complex*. Tensions at this stage can become resolved as children gradually identify with same-sex parents.

LATENCY STAGE (5/6 YEARS THROUGH TO PUBERTY)

At this stage, the libido really ceases being active. Freud suggested that during the latency stage sexual impulses become repressed and the sexual energy of children is redirected towards external activities such as sport and hobbies and, typically, peer friendships. Children's energies are now being channelled into developing their knowledge and skills and play is becoming increasingly evident with children of the same gender.

GENITAL STAGE (PUBERTY THROUGH TO ADULTHOOD)

The latency stage is followed by the genital stage. This is when adolescence is beginning and is often seen as a time when young people form identities and engage in experimentation.

ADAPTATIONS TO FREUD'S ORIGINAL THINKING

A number of key figures have adapted Freud's original ideas and in so doing have contributed much to our understanding of children's learning and social and emotional development. Four key figures are Erikson, Fromm, Isaacs and Neill; their adaptations of Freud's original theory have influenced thinking and practice in how we perceive and manage children's learning.

ERIK ERIKSON (1902–1994)

Erikson saw the course of normal development as moving through eight stages: *trust* versus *mistrust* (birth to 18 months); *autonomy* versus *shame* and *doubt* (1 to 3 years); *initiative* versus *guilt* (3 to 6 years); *industry* versus *inferiority* (6 to 12 years); *identity* versus *role confusion* (13–18 years); *intimacy* versus *isolation* (becoming a young adult); *generativity* versus *stagnation* (towards middle adulthood); *ego integrity* versus *despair* (old age). His theory is known as the 'theory of psychosocial development', which proposes that individuals who move successfully through each stage will achieve balanced and healthy personalities. When individuals do not, however, move through these stages successfully, they will develop personalities that can be unhealthy.

STAGE 1: TRUST VERSUS MISTRUST (BIRTH TO AROUND 18 MONTHS)

During this stage, children develop trust in the world around them and especially their carers. Trust is built

Natural activities can be the building blocks for independence and confidence

largely on the consistency and reliability of care that is given. If the care lacks these two elements, then children learn to mistrust and will carry this into future relationships, along with associated anxieties.

STAGE 2: AUTONOMY VERSUS SHAME AND DOUBT (1 TO AROUND 3 YEARS)

Children are now developing independence and autonomy. They have been learning to walk and are putting distance between themselves and their primary caregivers. Play is becoming increasingly important and is characterized increasingly by self-choice and interactions with others.

STAGE 3: INITIATIVE VERSUS GUILT (3 TO AROUND 6 YEARS)

Language is developing at a fast pace and children are acquiring the ability to empathize with others. Parents may restrict the activities of their children if they are concerned about potential risks. Too much restriction, punishment or excessive control may, however, result in feelings of guilt in their children, characterized in later years by a lack of initiative. Children typically engage in asking lots of questions. If requests for answers are not given appropriate status, then feelings of guilt accompanied by shame may ensue and lessen their desire to interact with their peers. Difficulties at this stage may be linked to the depression of creativity. At this stage, children are acquiring a sense of purpose.

STAGE 4: INDUSTRY VERSUS INFERIORITY (6 TO 12 YEARS)

Learning is becoming more sophisticated and more formal. Teachers and peer groups have become important role models and guide much of children's activities. Winning approval from peers is very important for it is through this that children can develop a sense of pride. Successful movement through this stage leads to children feeling industrious and confident in their ability to achieve. Unsuccessful movement can result in feelings of inferiority and doubt. At this stage, children develop their sense of competence.

ERICH FROMM (1900–1980)

Erich Fromm was a psychoanalyst and philosopher. Though prolific in his writing and adding much to our understanding of personal development in individuals, he offered what is a most intriguing account of the importance of 'love' in the lives of individuals (Fromm, 1975). Though writing some time ago, Fromm's theoretical framework of love still offers current practitioners a very helpful means for understanding the importance of love in the lives of young children. Fromm's theory focused on four elements central to 'love', which can be viewed as essential for children's holistic development. To be loved, he proposed, requires four key elements at the centre of our relationships, namely: *care*, *responsibility*, *respect* and *knowledge*. It is useful when considering the emotional needs of young children to reflect on the quality of each of these four elements in the lives of children; and how an absence of any of these is impacting on their development and their learning. How are young children being cared for, what level and type of responsibility is being shown to them by primary caregivers, how much respect are they given by those in their immediate environment and how much effort is made by their primary caregivers to build knowledge and understanding of their individual needs?

SUSAN ISAACS (1885–1948)

Susan Isaacs was born in Lancashire, England, and, having initially worked as an educationalist, she then entered the field of psychoanalysis. She has contributed a great deal to our understanding of early childhood, not only through her attempts at applying psychoanalytic thinking to children's learning, but also through her quite extensive writing (Isaacs, 1929, 1930, 1932). Isaacs saw the role of adults as central to children's learning, viewing them in terms of being a very valuable resource. At the heart of children's learning was, she argued, the need for them to develop their emotions and feelings; she saw children's learning environment as a necessary resource for the projection of their emotions and feelings. In this respect, she thought very much like Freud, who also viewed the environment as an important element in allowing individuals to project inner emotions and even, in some cases, unresolved issues such as anger. Children were set boundaries, which were demonstrated more than enforced and were promoted with a clear emphasis on consistency of approach by adults; this, she believed, was fundamental to their inner sense of security and safety. She saw the importance of adults having a detailed understanding of each individual child and believed that this could be achieved through careful and purposeful observation of the children in different situations. Isaacs also saw the benefits of teachers involving themselves and really getting into the worlds created by the children without impeding their natural

thinking, or interfering in it through, for example, listening patiently to children's talk and carefully observing their actions, behaviours and interests.

Isaacs believed passionately in the importance of nursery education and proposed how early years settings could reflect the warmth and love children ideally receive in their homes; they should also offer children new and motivating experiences that they might not otherwise have in their homes. She saw the nursery school as an extension of the home as opposed to being something separate. She felt that nursery school should offer children opportunities to develop socially and learn about relationships, which she argued were central to their emotional development. In 1924 Isaacs responded to an advertisement from Geoffrey and Margaret Pyke, who at the time wished to establish a nursery school for children aged between 2 and 7 years, based on new principles of learning and development, which later became known as the *Malting House School*. Isaacs created the Malting House School in such a way as to support children's physical and social development. Space was used in such a way as to stimulate children's thinking and learning through play. As with Montessori's furniture, it was small and adapted for young children. Places were allocated for quiet play and for rest, and resources were made available to help stimulate the children's learning and imagination, such as beads, blocks and soft materials. The main room opened to an outside area which included a playhouse, an area for gardening, a tool shed and a sandpit. Isaacs also believed strongly in the benefits that could be gained from taking children outside of the setting to experience other environments and activities.

Isaacs applied her training in psychoanalysis to develop her own understanding of the importance of play in children's learning and development, viewing play as a means of self-expression which enables children to express their true feelings and emotions in a safe way and, importantly, to have opportunities to engage in rehearsals of dealing with difficult emotions that they do not really understand. She suggested that play was central to children's very being; through play they could act out their fears and fantasies and in doing so would come to develop good mental wellbeing and positive personality traits.

Take time to read the following online article which explores the ideas and work of Susan Isaacs: 'Educational Pioneers: Susan Isaacs, 1885–1948', by Juliet Mickelburgh for the Early Years Foundation Stage

Forum (published 16.12.10): http://eyfs.info/articles.html/teaching-and-learning/educational-pioneers-susan-isaacs-1885–1948-r40.

ALEXANDER SUTHERLAND NEILL (1883–1973)

A.S. Neill worked primarily with school-aged children and is perhaps best known for his radical views on children's learning and education and the quite unique school that he opened, *Summerhill*. Neill's philosophical views on education and learning were much influenced by Freud and were located within the field of psychodynamics; he is largely associated with the idea of freeing children to learn in environments characterized by a lack of adult control. The influence of psychoanalysis on Neill's thinking can be seen clearly in the following extract from his own celebrated book, *Summerhill*:

> Freud showed that every neurosis is founded on sex repression. I said, 'I'll have a school in which there will be no sex repression'. Freud said that the unconscious was infinitely more important and more powerful than the conscious. I said, 'In my school we won't censure, punish, moralize. We will allow every child to live according to his deep impulses'. (1968, p. 20)

Neill (1968, p. 20) went on to offer the following quite controversial and much debated view of children's development: 'a child is innately wise and realistic. If left to himself without adult suggestion of any kind, he will develop as far as he is capable of developing'. With regard to children's education at Summerhill, he wrote that it offers an environment where 'lessons are optional … Children can go to them or stay away from them – for years if they want to'. Neill's views on education remain controversial and Summerhill school continues open today (see www.summerhillschool.co.uk).

WHAT THE THEORY LOOKS LIKE IN PRACTICE

Key elements of practice in early years settings can be observed to have their origins in the theoretical ideas of Freud and his followers. Practitioners work effectively to help children learn about relationships, to understand their inner emotions and to build strong feelings of trust and autonomy. They do this, for example, by placing emphasis on consistency in their approach, attending sensitively to children and demonstrating empathy. They take care to understand the tensions that children at different ages and stages may be experiencing and, importantly, they also take care to understand their own emotions and possible tensions as adults, through working closely with their peers and having good continuing professional development in place. Play is seen as having enormous potential to be therapeutic and to benefit those children who may live in homes where they have experienced neglect, poor attachment and even abuse. Play is used as a means by which children can work through emotionally difficult experiences, while at the same time feeling they are in a safe and secure environment.

STRENGTHS AND WEAKNESSES OF THE THEORY

Whilst much of Freud's original thinking and that of his followers continues to be celebrated and to influence practice, much criticism has also been levelled against

CASE STUDY: THE IMPORTANCE OF LOVE IN CHILDREN'S LIVES

Jess is 5 years of age and lives with her mother who is a registered Class A drug user and who has emotionally neglected Jess since birth. Jess has never met her father and, most nights, witnesses her mother becoming intoxicated by drugs or alcohol. On most weekends, her mother meets up with friends and goes out to clubs and bars, often not returning until well after midnight. Jess has to spend long periods of time alone and is undernourished. The family became known to social services following a referral made by the health visitor and paediatrician shortly after Jess's birth. Shortly after starting at nursery school, staff raised concerns with social services about Jess's poor state of dress and unkempt appearance most mornings, in addition to her apparent poor diet. They were particularly concerned about how Jess appeared to be very withdrawn, often being reluctant to play with other children and preferring to remain alongside adults, behaving most days in a 'clingy fashion' and an infantile way.

CASE STUDY: OFFERING SECURITY

Charlie is 3 years of age and recently lost his mother following a long illness. Adults working at his nursery school spend time with Charlie talking about his mother. He finds this very calming, even though he occasionally cries. Staff at the nursery meet each week with Charlie's father and talk through any upset they have observed in Charlie. In this way they feel they are not only offering support to Charlie but also to his family. His father is grateful that he can also talk to staff at the nursery school about any difficulties at home, such as Charlie's sleeping patterns and his eating habits. He feels very reassured by such meetings, which in turn impact positively on Charlie.

it. A primary criticism is that many of Freud's original ideas are not empirically verifiable. For example, how can we know that there is such a thing as an ego or that children move through such stages as the anal or phallic – what do these stages actually look like and are they the same for every child? How certain can we be that boys move through the Oedipus complex and girls through the Electra complex? These cannot be identified and his ideas cannot be measured.

LINKS TO OTHER THEORIES

Freud's theory is, in many respects, quite unique and has few similarities to other theorists. That said, there are many elements of his original ideas and those of his followers that can be located within the ideas of other theorists. Like early theorists such as Rousseau, Pestalozzi and Froebel, he valued the uniqueness of each child, and, like later theorists such as Dewey, Feuerstein and Noddings, he placed huge emphasis on the importance of children's emotional development being central to their learning experiences and development.

ACTIVITIES AND POINTS FOR DISCUSSION

Activity: Devise a list of activities you have observed young children engaging in and then identify what therapeutic value, if any, these had for the children.

Discussion Point: Consider the extent to which early years settings might feel compromised in their attempts to prioritize play and focus on creativity in light of external pressures from a government that focuses on 'standards'.

EXTENDED AND RECOMMENDED READING

Smith, L.A.H. (1985) *To Understand and to Help: The Life and Work of Susan Isaacs (1885–1948).* Plainsboro, NJ: Associated University Press.

Additional information on Sigmund Freud can be found at: www.freud.org.uk

REFERENCES

Fromm, E. (1975) *The Art of Loving.* London: Unwin Books.

Isaacs, S. (1929) *The Nursery Years.* London: Routledge.

Isaacs, S. (1930) *Intellectual Growth in Young Children.* London: Routledge.

Isaacs, S. (1932) *The Children We Teach.* London: University of London Press.

MacBlain, S.F. (2014) *How Children Learn.* London: Sage.

McLeod, S.A. (2008) Psychosexual Stages. Available at: www.simplypsychology.org/psychosexual.html (accessed 28.06.17).

Miller, L. and Pound, L. (2011) *Theories and Approaches to Learning in the Early Years.* London: Sage.

Neile, A.S. (1968) *Summerhill.* Harmondsworth: Pelican Books.

RUDOLF STEINER AND THE CHANGING NEEDS OF CHILDREN

THE THEORIST (1861–1925)

Rudolf Steiner founded his first school in the city of Stuttgart after being invited to do so by a wealthy industrialist, Emil Molt, who owned the Waldorf Astoria cigarette factory and who wanted a school where the children of his workers could be educated, hence the legacy by which Steiner schools have also come to be known as Steiner–Waldorf schools. Currently, there are more than a thousand Steiner schools and over 2000 early years settings across the world. Despite the original philosophy remaining constant, however, many of these schools and early years settings have developed in different ways.

KEY PUBLICATION

Steiner, R. (1907) *The Education of the Child*. East Grinstead: Anthroposophic Press.

UNDERSTANDING THE THEORY

Central to the Steiner–Waldorf tradition is the notion that young children learn through imitation. Adults model behaviours that children observe and that are beneficial to their learning; imitation is seen as a natural process in children's development. Miller and Pound (2011, p. 88) have encapsulated this aspect of Steiner–Waldorf practice as follows: 'and whatever is happening around the child becomes part of that child as she absorbs not only the outer actions of the adults, but the inner attitudes too'. Also central to this tradition is the importance of the relationships that are established and maintained between practitioners and children, which are viewed as important in developing children's learning. Steiner saw the fundamental purpose of education as being that of responding to the evolving intellectual and emotional needs of children. Central to his philosophy are the following key points:

Learning is a natural and creative process that benefits from structure

- In the first years and up to age 7, a high level of emphasis is given to play and art, including drawing and the natural world of children, with links being made between art and the sciences.

- Prior to age 7, children are not taught reading in a formal way, the rationale being that children will naturally learn to read anyway, provided their social and emotional development has been positive. This is also the case with mathematics where children are introduced to formal mathematics at a later stage.

- Interestingly, Steiner's philosophy proposes that children should be taught writing before reading.

- Children are encouraged to sing each day and to learn how to play musical instruments.

- Children learn to create individual lesson books within which they write and illustrate.

- An additional feature of Steiner schools is how teachers use a narrative approach to their children's learning. They place much emphasis on listening with children being encouraged to develop their imagination. An example of this is where children are introduced to new material through a story and are then supported by the teacher with revisiting the content of the story in the following days and encouraged to retell the story. The objective is to develop children's spoken language, in addition to extending memory capacity. Children are then supported with recording their stories in written form.

Nicol (2010, pp. 85–6) has drawn attention to key features underpinning the practice of kindergarten teachers in Steiner–Waldorf schools, where children's learning is viewed very much in terms of it being a continuous process. In so doing, practitioners apply patience to waiting as the process of learning in each child unfolds, applying 'insight' rather than measurement. A key question at the heart of this process is 'Who are you?' rather than 'What can you do?' Nicol has also indicated how kindergarten teachers at Steiner–Waldorf schools refrain from rushing children's 'natural speed of development'; instead, the teacher 'meditates on the child, holds the child in his/her thoughts (a process termed as "inner work")'. Importantly, assessment of learning takes place largely through observation by teachers, with a particular focus on social and emotional development.

WHAT THE THEORY LOOKS LIKE IN PRACTICE

Where possible, children in Steiner settings have the same teacher throughout their primary years and in so doing learn to value the importance of relationships. This continuity allows their teachers to acquire greater knowledge of their pupils' social and emotional development. Routines are also considered important as are the benefits gained through repetition of activities and the importance of rhythm. Miller and Pound (2011, p. 92) have commented on how children

in Steiner–Waldorf settings become 'nurtured by the security of rhythm and repetition'. Miller and Pound go on to emphasize how in these settings, 'having well thought through and repeated routines build habits that are useful (properly washed hands), respectful (creating a peaceful mood at the table) and comforting ("this is how we always do it here")'.

It is possible to observe many of the ideas that are central to Steiner's theory being applied by practitioners in early years settings. We can, for example, see imitation in children's learning experiences, with adults taking care to actively observe children and refrain from hurrying or rushing them in their natural development. This is of course quite different from delaying children in their development. Reflective practitioners who understand the principles put forward by Steiner will be sensitive to how children learn, the rate at which they can best learn and the types of activities and environments that facilitate natural learning. I (the author) was fortunate enough to visit a Steiner setting some years ago and was very taken by the enormous sense of calm throughout the setting and the relaxed atmosphere in which the children and adults worked closely alongside each other.

Practitioners in early years settings take care to model behaviours that children can imitate and learn from, which is key to Steiner's thinking. In this way, they extend opportunities for children to form and develop purposeful relationships with adults that encourage strong emotional growth. Most, if not all, early years settings promote routines that are meaningful and that provide a strong sense of security for the children. Everywhere, creativity is encouraged together with an appreciation of the natural world. In very young children, 'mark making' is encouraged as a precursor to writing, with some settings acknowledging Steiner's emphasis on writing being taught before reading.

STRENGTHS AND WEAKNESSES OF THE THEORY

The influence of Rudolf Steiner on our understanding and delivery of education has been substantial (MacBlain, 2014). There are some, however, who hold a less favourable view of his ideas, which have continued to be controversial in some quarters. He has even been referred to as 'a maverick Austrian scientist' (Edwards, 2002, p. 2). Criticisms have been raised over the late onset of literacy in some children and the fact that the education of children attending these schools lies to some extent outside of what is viewed as practice in most mainstream settings.

CASE STUDY: SUPPORTING EMOTIONAL DEVELOPMENT THROUGH CONTINUITY AND STRUCTURE

Beth is aged 5 years and has just enrolled in a Steiner–Waldorf school. Beth's parents are excited by the new opportunities they feel she will be offered. They are keen that she develops socially and emotionally and is encouraged to develop her own creativity and sense of well-being. They are also keen that Beth learns the importance of structure in her life. As Beth settles into her new school, her parents become increasingly aware of the importance that the adults working with Beth place on imitation and repetition, and the predictable arrangements for each day's activities. They observe Beth to be gaining emotionally through a developing sense of continuity to her day. They feel this is adding to her self-confidence and building on her self-efficacy.

CASE STUDY: LEARNING THROUGH A CHILD'S NATURAL ENVIRONMENT

Arthur is aged 5 and attends a Steiner–Waldorf school. Staff working with Arthur encourage him to develop his early literacy skills through, for example, observing and attending to words in his natural environment. Arthur is delighted when he can read words to his parents that he sees as they drive in their car and go on shopping trips.

LINKS TO OTHER THEORIES

Like other theorists such as Pestalozzi and Rousseau, Steiner paid particular attention to the sensitive nature of childhood, the importance of forming and developing relationships and the expanse of opportunities for developing children's creativity. In these respects, his ideas link well to those of Froebel and later theorists such as Montessori, Bruner and Noddings, and many of the ideas that have underpinned practice in the Reggio Emilio approach. Like other theorists, Steiner placed particular emphasis on the importance of the senses and in this way his ideas were very similar to those of Montessori and, indeed, later theorists such as Dewey, Noddings and Bronfenbrenner. It is interesting to reflect on how relevant Steiner's ideas remain for those children who experience different types of special educational needs and/or disabilities such as autism or attentional deficit disorder (ADD).

EXTENDED AND RECOMMENDED READING

Nicol, J. (2016) *Bringing the Steiner Waldorf Approach to Your Early Years Practice*. London: Routledge.

REFERENCES

Edwards, C. (2002) 'Three approaches from Europe: Waldorf, Montessori, and Reggio Emilia', *Early Childhood, Research and Practice*, 4(1): 1–14.

MacBlain, S.F. (2014) *How Children Learn*. London: Sage.

Miller, L. and Pound, L. (2011) *Theories and Approaches to Learning in the Early Years*. London: Sage.

Nicol, J. (2010) *Bringing the Steiner Waldorf Approach to Your Early Years Practice*. London: Routledge.

ACTIVITIES AND POINTS FOR DISCUSSION

Activity: Identify examples where you have observed children imitating adults' behaviours. List some of the specific behaviours as well as examples of the language used by adults that children have imitated.

Discussion Point: How might the Steiner–Waldorf approach support young children with attachment disorders and children on the autistic spectrum?

MARIA MONTESSORI: THE ENVIRONMENT AND LEARNING

THE THEORIST (1870–1952)

Maria Montessori was born in Italy and was the first woman in her country to become a doctor. Maria was a single parent and at 13 years of age chose to attend a single-sex school for boys as a way of educating herself to take up a career as an engineer. Her contribution to how we understand learning in young children and early child development has been immense and continues to be recognized throughout the world. Montessori took a special interest in trying to understand the needs of those children with learning difficulties, who, at the time, were generally considered to be uneducable. She had considerable success with these children and was appointed director of the *Scuola Ortofrenica*, one of a number of institutions in Italy which looked after children with mental health problems.

KEY PUBLICATION

Montessori, M. (1912) *The Montessori Method*. London: Heinemann.

Experience supports children in learning to become independent

UNDERSTANDING THE THEORY

At the core of Montessori's theory is the notion of 'planes', or stages, through which children pass as they learn. Montessori proposed 11 'sensitive' periods within the first stage or plane (0 to 6 years): Movement; Language; Small Objects; Order; Music; Grace and Courtesy; Refinement of the Senses; Writing Fascination; Reading; Spatial Relationships; and Mathematics (see Gray and MacBlain, 2015, pp. 186–7, for a discussion of these periods). She suggested that it is when moving through the first 'plane' that children first experience significant change in their social and emotional development, as well as in their physical development. During this stage, infants, for example, take their first steps, use their first words and start to engage actively with those around them, and between the ages of 1 and 4 they can be observed to fixate on objects and on detail; this is very important for their development, which facilitates growth in attention and concentration. It is during this stage that children develop their memory and there is an enormous spurt in using and understanding language.

By the time children are ready to move into the second plane, they can run and jump and are engaging in conversations with other children and adults. Language has become more complex and sophisticated and they are beginning to experience and understand their own feelings as well as those of others. During this stage, they are learning to adapt their own behaviours and actions in response to others' feelings and their environment. Friendships are being formed and they are learning how to adapt to the often complex nature of those social interactions they experience within their family and in their early years settings.

Montessori suggested that between 2 and 6 years of age children demonstrate a natural interest in music, for example singing, rhythm and beat. She also suggested that children at this age display what she referred to as 'grace and courtesy' and a 'refinement of the senses' when they can be observed, for example, imitating the more refined behaviours of others, most typically adults and older siblings. In so doing, these refined behaviours then become internalized within the children's own cognitive structures. At around 3–4 years, children can be observed to display a much greater interest in sensory stimuli such as taste and touch. During this stage, they also, Montessori believed, display a much greater interest in writing and can be seen trying to copy written symbols such as letters and numbers and even words. An interest in reading also becomes evident between the ages of 3 and 5 years when children can be observed showing interest in the sounds that letters make and how written words are spoken. Between 4 and 6 years of age, children demonstrate

an interest in spatial relationships and begin to map out the environments around them, for example gardens, the street where they live, local supermarkets where their parents shop, parks, and so on. They also begin to develop abilities with solving puzzles, such as jigsaws. Basic concepts in mathematical thinking using concrete materials are developed during this period. It is during the second plane that children's learning and thinking become more abstract as they are beginning to go beyond just simply reacting to sensory stimuli. Thinking is, therefore, becoming much more complex.

Montessori promoted the idea of independence and the importance of children learning to look after themselves as well as their environments. One can

Young children display a natural interest in copying written symbols

Mathematical thinking is supported by the imaginative use of concrete materials

observe, for example, children in Montessori nurseries involved in tasks such as dressing themselves and tidying the areas in which they both play and learn. Montessori also promoted the idea that children should develop at their own pace and be encouraged to incorporate within their thinking a belief that learning is enjoyable.

Children's natural interests can serve as key motivators in their learning

REPETITION

Montessori believed strongly in the importance of repetition being central to children's learning and as an important means of laying down the foundations for more abstract learning. Montessori did not, however, advocate the learning of new skills through the repetition of activities that were uninteresting to children. Rather, she proposed the repetition of tasks and activities that promote creative thinking and learning and stimulate over-learning, which leads to the internalization of new concepts and deeper understanding. As new concepts are introduced to children, a three-step process develops: the introduction of new ideas; understanding these in concrete terms; and then understanding them in abstract terms. Teaching, she proposed, should be individualized and should place significant emphasis on developing children's observational skills through all of their five senses.

It is of note that many of Montessori's ideas correspond to the requirements of the current Early Years Foundation Stage (EYFS), which frames and informs practice in the UK. Indeed, Miller and Pound (2011, p. 81) have drawn attention to how supporters of the Montessori principles have engaged with the Office for Standards in Education (Ofsted) in the UK and local authorities to encourage the use of approaches in working with young children that are grounded in the original ideas of Montessori. That said, it is worth pointing out that Montessori teachers are not, in fact, eligible to teach in state schools within the UK (MacBlain, 2014).

THE IMPORTANCE OF OBSERVATION

Commenting on the importance of observation in the classroom, Feez (2010, p. 24) has indicated how those training to become Montessori teachers are encouraged to sit quietly in a place where they will not distract the children, and to record even the smallest of details, for example:

- everything that interests each child, no matter how apparently insignificant
- how long a child sustains interest in each activity they choose, whether for seconds, minutes or hours
- how a child moves, especially movement of the hand
- how many times a child repeats the same activity
- how a child interacts with others.

As trainee practitioners engage in detailed observations, they come to better understand children's behaviours and learning. Their interpretations of children's behaviours and the meanings they attach to these behaviours also become clearer and more accurate. This then leads to them having much better insight into the nature of each child's holistic learning and development.

WHAT THE THEORY LOOKS LIKE IN PRACTICE

Many of Montessori's original principles remain with us even today and one can find her influence almost everywhere. Montessori, for example, introduced us to the notion of the *Casa dei Bambini*, or *Children's House*, in which teachers create environments that stimulate children, where they are unrestricted in their learning and where learning can be individual and natural. In her attention to detail and her lasting focus on 'getting it right' for children, she even designed special furniture for the Children's Houses; this can be seen in many early years settings. Montessori was also a strong advocate of the principle that much of children's learning should be through their senses, and she believed that a core feature of education should be the need for children to take significant responsibility for their own learning. Such features are now to be found almost everywhere in early years practice, where one can observe practitioners actively encouraging children to be independent and take responsibility for aspects of their own learning.

Readers should take time to view the following YouTube link entitled 'Montessori Sensorial Exercises' (posted on 27 December 2010), which offers clear and accessible insights into the principles

CASE STUDY: THE POWER OF OBSERVATION – ATTRIBUTING MEANING TO BEHAVIOURS

Maria has just started her first placement as a student in a local playgroup. She is very aware that there are a range of abilities amongst the children as well as a range of socioeconomic backgrounds. She has been tasked by the lecturers on her degree course to take time to develop her observational skills. Maria finds a quiet corner in the room where she will not distract the children who have previously shown a great deal of interest in her as she is a 'new' face in their environment. Maria takes time to observe two children and makes detailed notes on such behaviours as how they interact with others, the extent to which they initiate conversations with other children, and how they cooperate and collaborate with other children in play activities. On her return to her degree course, she spends time talking with her lecturer about her observations and finds that she is able to objectively discuss the behaviours she has recorded and interpret these using her new knowledge of theory.

CASE STUDY: LEARNING TO CARE FOR THEIR ENVIRONMENT

Maria has more recently embarked on her second placement in a nursery school and has been tasked by her university tutors with identifying any aspects of children's learning that can be traced back to Montessori's original principles. She observes each day how the children are encouraged to care for their learning environment by helping with tidying up after engaging in activities. Maria notes that this emphasis on caring for their environment supports the children in developing a greater sense of independence. She also observes how staff at the nursery encourage the children to develop their skills in dressing themselves, noting how this also supports the children in developing their independence, which is a key element in Montessori's theory.

underpinning Montessori practice and, in particular, the emphasis Montessori placed on sensory learning and how this facilitates observation and concentration in children (www.youtube.com/watch?v=NlnHVxJKEiM [accessed 26.07.17]).

Now look at the two case studies, which illustrate aspects of the thinking that underpins Montessori's theoretical principles.

STRENGTHS AND WEAKNESSES OF THE THEORY

Whilst Montessori's ideas have been celebrated by many practitioners, some have challenged aspects of her thinking. Holt (1967, p. 243), for example, proposed in the 1960s how Montessori and many of her followers did not approve of children fantasizing, acknowledging, however, that, 'Of course some Montessori people disagree with this'. Holt, nonetheless, voiced his opinion that, 'I think they are much mistaken'. More recently, Miller and Pound (2011, p. 81) commented on how, in 2008, over 80 per cent of Montessori nurseries had been viewed by Ofsted as good or outstanding. They also indicated that whilst local authorities had the power to oversee and monitor the quality of EYFS provision for 3- and 4-year-olds, their interpretations of the EYFS could, in fact, vary between local authorities and could 'easily ignore the particular nature of Montessori education'.

LINKS TO OTHER THEORIES

Like Piaget, Montessori saw children's learning and thinking as developing through stages. In common with Piaget, Bruner and Vygotsky, she also viewed learning very much as a social activity. Unlike the behaviourists, she placed great emphasis on the feelings and emotions experienced by children and how these, together with their senses, impacted on their learning. In this respect, she was very similar in her thinking to later theorists such as Bandura, Bronfenbrenner, Dewey and Noddings. Montessori offered practitioners at the time a means of giving much greater clarity to the holistic development of young children, especially those from disadvantaged backgrounds and those with special needs. View the YouTube video, 'Early Childhood Education, Froebel and Montessori': www.youtube.com/watch?v=OLcKTB_aAFs, which explores the similarities between Montessori's ideas and those of Froebel.

> ### ACTIVITIES AND POINTS FOR DISCUSSION
>
> **Activity:** View the YouTube video entitled 'Montessori Vs. Conventional School', available at www.youtube.com/watch?v=3NGRpzQ9vCE, and identify the key differences between Montessori learning settings and conventional settings.
>
> **Discussion Point:** Consider why those who have been trained as Montessori teachers are not permitted to teach in UK state schools. Should this be reversed?

EXTENDED AND RECOMMENDED READING

Gray, C. and MacBlain, S.F. (2015) *Learning Theories in Childhood* (2nd edn). London: Sage.

Lea, S. (2013) 'Early years work, professionalism and the translation of policy into practice', in Z. Kingdon and J. Gourd (eds), *Early Years Policy: The Impact on Practice*. London: Routledge. (An interesting and challenging chapter focusing on professionalism in early years practice.)

REFERENCES

Feez, S. (2010) *Montessori and Early Childhood*. London: Sage.

Gray, C. and MacBlain, S.F. (2015) *Learning Theories in Childhood* (2nd edn). London: Sage.

Holt, J. (1967) *How Children Learn*. Harmondsworth: Penguin.

MacBlain, S.F. (2014) *How Children Learn*. London: Sage.

Miller, L. and Pound, L. (2011) *Theories and Approaches to Learning in the Early Years*. London: Sage.

PART SUMMARY

As stressed at the beginning of this text, it is fundamental that we view the ideas of theorists and philosophers within the historical context in which they live. Doing so provides us with insights into why they developed their thinking and the factors that influenced them at the time. All theorists view aspects of children's learning differently and whilst none are completely wrong, none are also completely right. We should not look for one theory that explains all aspects of children's learning; instead, we should examine what theorists suggest and take from their theories those aspects that help us in our understanding of children's learning and wider social and emotional development.

We now turn to more recent thinkers who, in building on the ideas of the early theorists and philosophers, have contributed further to our understanding of children's learning in what has been a rapidly changing and increasingly complex world.

PART 2

MODERN INFLUENCES

Practitioners today have not only benefitted from the ideas of theorists and philosophers over the generations, they have also gained from practice that has challenged the thinking of its time and created learning environments for young children that have served as excellent examples of what is possible, even in times of economic, political and social strife.

Children's learning in early years settings reflects the considerable expertise and creativity of practitioners

JOHN DEWEY AND CHILD-CENTRED EDUCATION

THE THEORIST (1859–1952)

John Dewey was born in the USA and is most often associated with the concept of child-centred education. Whilst his ideas were much loved by many they were also disliked by others as indicated by the American philosopher Nell Noddings (2005), cited by the British philosopher Richard Pring who indicated how some had felt that Dewey's ideas were detrimental to children's education because he had, in effect, replaced 'true' education with too much of an emphasis on 'socialization'. Pring also cited an incident when he was with Lord Keith Joseph, then, Secretary of State for Education under Prime Minister Margaret Thatcher who had accused him of being largely responsible for most of the problems in schools because he had introduced teachers to the ideas of Dewey (Pring, 2007, p.3).

KEY PUBLICATION

Dewey, J. and Dewey, E. (1915) *Schools of Tomorrow*. London: E.P. Dutton & Co.

UNDERSTANDING THE THEORY

To assess Dewey's theory properly, one must understand the world into which he was born and grew up. Queen Victoria still ruled over the British Empire and the practice of baby farming, where newly born infants were 'farmed out' to women who looked after them, was still rife (MacBlain, 2014). Dewey was born in the same year as the infamous outlaw 'Billy the Kid' and lived through both world wars. He developed his ideas on learning at a time when education was typically highly formal, with children being expected to attend school and simply 'absorb' information. Ask any adult who attended school in the 1950s and 1960s and it is likely they will recall days at school spent sitting in silence in regimented rows waiting to have questions directed at them by their

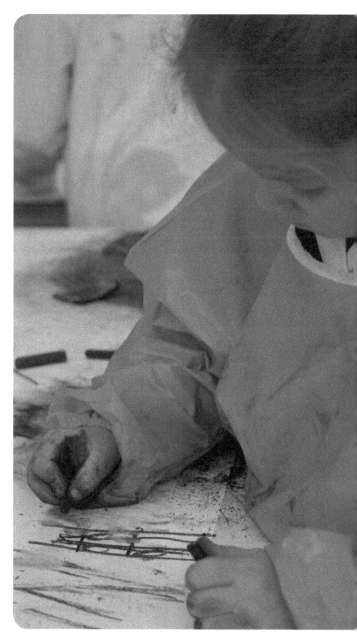

Each child's learning is a unique and individual process

teachers. Dewey's ideas on learning should, therefore, be viewed against this backdrop. In contrast to the education of the day, Dewey emphasized the importance of understanding children's experiences and how these impacted on their learning. He argued that education should be viewed as a means of preparing children to be effective members of the societies in which they lived and to be valued by their communities. In essence, Dewey saw education and democracy as being intertwined and fundamental to one another.

Dewey was controversial in his views about what schools should look like and challenged much of the thinking of his time, which supported passive learning where children attended schools and early years settings that were typically defined by rules, strict codes of behaviour, lessons that were, on the whole, undertaken in silence with often only the teacher talking and an exaggerated emphasis on memorizing information.

SUPPORTING CHILDREN'S LEARNING

Dewey believed strongly that children require support from adults with structuring their learning. He saw the role of the teacher very much as that of being a guide and a facilitator of new learning and new experiences. How they created these new experiences was, he argued, key to effective learning. Dewey also believed strongly in the uniqueness of every child, which he believed was formed through their experiences, as well as genetically. Dewey believed that children engage differently with the curricula they receive in their schools, and argued that the curricula offered by schools should take into account the individual nature of how each child learns and actively work to support differences in how they learn.

THE IMPORTANCE OF EXPERIENCE

Dewey proposed that experience was central to children's learning and the transmission of knowledge. He suggested that experiences have no attached value in themselves, but, rather, it is what each child takes from the experience that is important for learning. No two children will encounter and learn from experiences in precisely the same way. What will benefit one child may be of little use to another. Dewey believed that when teachers have a better understanding of children's past experiences, they can then become better informed as to how to shape their learning through new experiences that are structured and that build on their existing knowledge.

WHAT THE THEORY LOOKS LIKE IN PRACTICE

Dewey is often associated with student-led learning. His legacy has been embraced by many and he has influenced thinking and practice across a range of settings. Dewey encouraged teachers to develop their own interests, which he argued then impact positively on their teaching. He is also often reported as being a strong advocate of project work, where children's learning involves working on particular topic areas or collaborative activities that can then be facilitated and developed by their teachers. Much of Dewey's thinking about learning was drawn from his 'laboratory schools', which he first established in Chicago in 1896 for children from nursery age through to 12th grade. Here, he could observe and test his ideas on learning. Pring (2007, p. 16) stressed how Dewey's experimental school had demonstrated the importance of taking children's curiosity and interests into account when designing curricula in schools.

Pring also indicated how Dewey saw the school as an extension of the home and of children's communities; they should value 'manual and practical activity' (2007, pp. 15–17) as well as the interests of the children,

CASE STUDY: THE EXPERIENCE OF LEARNING IS UNIQUE TO EACH CHILD

Oscar and Jasmine are both 5 years of age and are in the first year of schooling. Their teacher has recently become anxious that the school might have to undergo an inspection. She has been instructed by her head teacher to concentrate on teaching phonics to her class as this is an area that the inspectors might want to focus on, should they come. She decides that she will teach certain phonetic sounds to the whole class each day. Oscar and Jasmine report back to their parents at the end of each day that they have been learning the sounds of letters and letter blends. Jasmine's mother is delighted as she feels Jasmine is now learning how to read as she started school not knowing any sounds and not being able to say her alphabet. Oscar's mother, on the other hand, is not happy and makes an appointment to see Oscar's teacher. She stresses to Oscar's teacher that Oscar started school being able to read very well and can write and correctly spell a range of words. She sees the teaching of new sounds to Oscar as a waste of his time.

CASE STUDY: SUPPORTING LEARNING THROUGH EXPERIENCE

It is the start of a new week and the playgroup leader has decided to introduce the children to a new activity, which she hopes will improve their understanding of colour and develop their thinking or underlying cognitive processes regarding categorization. She has invited some parents to come along and assist, making a ratio of one adult to every three children. The children are given large pieces of white paper and different coloured paints and told simply to 'draw a picture using lots of colour'. As they begin, the adults in the room mingle and talk the children through what they are doing, telling them the names of the colours they are using and then supporting their learning by encouraging the children to mix different colours to make new colours and then naming these. The children repeat the names of the colours and new colours and excitedly tell their peers which colours they have made and the names of these. In this way, the adults have supported new learning through experience.

which he claimed should be treated as important and relevant to children's learning. Dewey suggested that when the interests of children are taken seriously by teachers and when teachers seek to develop these interests in children, then the children will be 'disciplined by the pursuit of those interests – making the regime of externally imposed discipline irrelevant'. It must be remembered, of course, that, at the time, most children in primary school typically sat in rows and in silence for most of the day. It was also the case that early years education was very poorly understood and very poorly resourced.

LINKS TO OTHER THEORIES

Like Piaget, Bruner and Vygotsky, Dewey saw learning very much as a social activity in which children should be active participants. Like Piaget, he placed considerable emphasis on the importance of the environment and how experience impacts on learning. Unlike the behaviourists, he concerned himself with those processes inside children's minds that they can bring to new learning. Like Bruner, Dewey saw the teacher as playing a crucial role in guiding children's learning.

STRENGTHS AND WEAKNESSES OF THE THEORY

A frequently voiced misconception about Dewey's theory of education is that he promoted learning that was, essentially, student-led. To the contrary, he believed strongly that children's learning at school should be guided by a clear structure. A major strength of Dewey's theory was that it shifted the emphasis away from children simply absorbing information to becoming more active participants in their own learning. His theory also shifted thinking at the time in regard to the role of the teacher being more of a facilitator to children's learning.

Children's learning environments can now be much more informal

ACTIVITIES AND POINTS FOR DISCUSSION

Activity: Look at the YouTube video clip entitled 'John Dewey Experience and Education: a brief summary': www.youtube.com/watch?v=zwlcl-G93Mo (A. Wisdom), and then consider the following: Given the ease with which children and even very young children can access information through the internet, should they be given more freedom to learn independently?

Discussion Point: Are those who advocate for a return to more formal and traditional teaching, as was the case when Dewey was originally developing his theories, misguided?

EXTENDED AND RECOMMENDED READING

Gray, C. and MacBlain, S.F. (2015) *Learning Theories in Childhood* (2nd edn). London: Sage.

Ryan, M. and Bourke, T. (2013) 'The teacher as reflexive professional: making visible the excluded discourse in teacher standards', *Discourse: Studies in the Cultural Politics of Education*, 34(3): 411–23. (An interesting account of the relevance of 'teachers' standards' to practice in school.)

REFERENCES

MacBlain, S.F. (2014) *How Children Learn*. London: Sage.

Noddings, N. (2005) 'Caring in education', in *The Encyclopaedia of Informal Education*. Available at: http://infed.org/mobi/caring-in-education (accessed 06.11.17).

Pring, R. (2007) *John Dewey: A Philosopher of Education for Our Time*? London: Continuum International Publishing Group.

BURRHUS SKINNER AND THE BEHAVIOURISTS

THE THEORIST (1904–1990)

Burrhus Skinner is regarded by many as the primary figure in the field of *behaviourism*, which arose from the early work of Ivan Pavlov, progressing through that of Edward Thorndike and, later, John Watson. Skinner undertook much of his work within laboratory settings where he experimented with animals, most often rats. He was especially interested in exploring the effects of reinforcement on the behaviour of these animals, and how this might be applied to understanding human behaviour.

KEY PUBLICATIONS

Skinner, B.F. (1951) *How to Teach Animals*. San Francisco, CA: W.H. Freeman.

Skinner, B.F. (1953) *Science and Human Behavior*. New York: Simon & Schuster.

UNDERSTANDING THE THEORY

Behaviourism is premised on the view that associations develop between stimuli and responses and that these account for learning (MacBlain, 2014). Drawing on the original notion of 'empiricism', which originated with the philosopher John Locke, behaviourists proposed that learning could be observed, examined and explained in a systematic and objective manner and with little consideration being afforded to inner emotions and feelings. Behaviourism came to dominate much practice in education in previous decades and, in many respects, was a reaction to the earlier ideas of the psychodynamic theorists such as Freud, Klein and Erikson. Any exploration of behaviourism needs to begin with the original work of the Russian physiologist Ivan Pavlov, whose experiments with animals formed a starting point for the behaviourists in seeking to develop a theory, along scientific principles that would explain learning. Pavlov's theory came to be known as *classical conditioning*.

IVAN PAVLOV (1849–1936) AND CLASSICAL CONDITIONING

Pavlov observed during his early experiments with dogs how they salivated when one of his assistants came into the room in which they were housed. He noticed particularly that the dogs salivated even when the assistants did not bring food with them and that even their entry into the room was enough to make them salivate. He referred to this behaviour in the dogs as 'associated learning', suggesting that the dogs had established an association between the assistant entering the room and being fed. Pavlov then set about training the dogs to respond to different associations – for example, ringing a bell when food was introduced to the dogs and then observing them salivating at the mere sound of the bell. Pavlov's ideas were taken further by Edward Thorndike who attempted to apply them to understanding how children learn.

EDWARD THORNDIKE (1874–1954) AND LEARNING BY ASSOCIATION

Thorndike suggested that much learning occurs through trial and error and that if outcomes of learning activities were positive, then connections would be formed which would lead to the repetition of behaviours. Thorndike developed an experiment in which he attempted to examine those laws that he believed underpinned learning. In one of his experiments, he put a hungry cat in a box, designed in such a way as to let the cat see a fish outside of the box. He observed how the cat tried to escape from the box in order to eat the fish. On each occasion that the cat escaped from the box, he was returned to it. To begin with, the cat's attempts at escaping were of a trial and error nature. As time progressed, however, the cat became quicker at escaping because it was making a connection between how to escape and a lever on the box, which, when pressed, opened the door. Thorndike saw this process of learning within the cat as moving initially from random acts to more deliberate attempts by the cat to use its paw to push the lever – he referred to this as the 'Law of Effect'.

He suggested then that acts that result in positive outcomes increase. He also suggested, however, that acts resulting in negative behaviours and that produce undesirable or non-pleasurable results become weaker and eventually disappear.

JOHN WATSON (1878–1954) AND THE EMERGENCE OF BEHAVIOURISM

In 1913 John Watson established the school of 'behaviourism', which was based on the view that all behaviours are acquired through the process of conditioning. Though Thorndike had drawn on Pavlov's earlier ideas and offered some rudimentary insights into how learning took place, Watson was really the first theorist to extend Pavlov's original ideas based on observations of animals, to that of understanding learning in humans. Watson's confidence in the contribution that behaviourism could make to our understanding of learning in children can be seen in an often quoted statement by Watson that, given a healthy young child in their early years and his own specifications of their learning environments he could 'train' them to become any type of specialist when they were grown up (Watson, 1928, p. 82).

B.F. SKINNER (1904–1990) AND OPERANT CONDITIONING

Drawing on the work of Watson, B.F. Skinner recognized how reinforcement that is positive strengthens the behaviours of individuals. Importantly, Skinner also observed how the frequency with which reinforcement followed behavioural responses was an important factor in increasing behaviours. In developing this idea, he proposed a number of schedules of reinforcement, which have informed the practice of many teachers and early years practitioners in seeking to change the behaviours of children presenting with behavioural issues and conduct disorders. Skinner developed the idea of operant conditioning, based on his proposition that learning was not wholly a passive process, as had been considered by the early behaviourists, but rather an active process. In contrast to classical conditioning, operant conditioning holds that it is the learner and not the object that triggers changes in behaviour. With operant conditioning, learning takes place when behaviours are either rewarded or punished and when, in effect, associations are formed between behaviours and the consequences of those behaviours. Skinner observed that behaviour could be shaped and then sustained by its consequences. He suggested, for example, that pleasant responses strengthen behaviours and unpleasant responses weaken behaviours, with the result that they tend to diminish. Put simply, positive reinforcement strengthens learning whilst negative reinforcement diminishes it.

Interestingly, Skinner, like many later behaviourists, came to view computers as one of the most effective means of learning for children. By using computers, children could, he suggested, follow carefully designed programmes, which could, at each new stage of learning, offer appropriate and effective reinforcement through rewards. They could also break learning down into small steps, which would lessen the possibility of children experiencing failure and increase the degree of success and, thereby, the effective reinforcement of learning.

Gray and MacBlain (2015, p. 59) have commented on how Skinner believed that teachers should be knowledgeable and should approach their work with children having a clear plan as to how they should deliver material. In this way, teachers can, Skinner argued, be in a much better position to reinforce responses by children that are accurate and, in so doing, actively 'shape' their learning.

CASE STUDY: CLASSICAL CONDITIONING IN ACTION

Miss Barker is a newly qualified teacher and it is her first day with a Key Stage 1 class. She has decided to introduce a method for signalling the children to be quiet. She rings a small bell and tells her class that when they hear the bell they must sit up straight, fold their arms and stop talking. After a week or so, the children have formed an association with the bell and it is now enough for Miss Barker to just reach for the bell and to hold it in the air before the children fold their arms and stop talking.

CASE STUDY: OPERANT CONDITIONING IN ACTION

Mrs Crawford has taken over working with a new Key Stage 1 class as their regular teacher is ill. She has been told that a child named Will is frequently the cause of low-level disruption in the classroom. He spends much of his time trying to distract the other children and, on most occasions, does not begin to attempt the work set for the whole class. Mrs Crawford decides to try an intervention that she hopes will extinguish Will's undesirable behaviours and replace them with desirable behaviours. She believes that the main reason for Will's undesirable behaviours is his need for greater attention. On the next day, Mrs Crawford sets the whole class a simple and enjoyable task, which requires minimal effort. She notes that Will becomes quickly absorbed in the task and appears to be quite motivated. She goes straight to Will whilst he is absorbed in the task and speaks clearly and softly to Will, explaining to him that she is very pleased with his behaviour, which is 'working quietly' and 'being attentive' to what is being asked of him. She smiles at him and then walks away. After a few minutes, she goes back to Will and again explains to him that she is very pleased with his behaviour, which is 'working quietly' and 'being attentive' to what he is doing. After 10 minutes or so, she stops the class doing the activity and calls for attention. She emphasizes how pleased she is and especially emphasizes that she is pleased with the children's behaviour, which is 'working quietly' and 'being attentive'. In this way, she is, once again, identifying those behaviours she is seeking to reinforce in Will. Later on in the morning session, she calls Will over to her desk and again explains that she is very pleased with his behaviour, which is 'working quietly' and 'being attentive'. Mrs Crawford continues to reinforce Will's desired behaviours by repeating this approach each day with different tasks; by the end of the second week, she has noted a significant change in Will's behaviour. She concludes that rather than giving Will attention when he is being disruptive, she will give him attention when he is actively engaged in a task and reinforce his 'on-task' behaviours through smiles and verbal encouragement.

WHAT THE THEORY LOOKS LIKE IN PRACTICE

The principles of behaviourism can be evidenced daily in classrooms and early years settings, though, mostly, this happens at a sub-conscious level. Early years practitioners and teachers regularly offer stimuli to children and reinforce their behaviours often without being fully aware of what they are doing. Positive reinforcement between a teacher and a child might, for example, include the teacher's smiles or verbal praise. A common practice in many classrooms and early years settings is that of placing stars on a star chart when a pupil has successfully completed a task or demonstrated a desired behaviour. In order to gain a star, the child needs to demonstrate a behaviour desired by one of the adults in the room. Examples of negative reinforcement, on the other hand, can also be observed in classrooms where teachers may use 'time out' for a child who is presenting with unacceptable behaviours. Practitioners employ, on a daily basis, positive reinforcement to increase desired behaviours and negative reinforcement to discourage or extinguish undesirable behaviours. Many practitioners and primary teachers will be familiar with the use of such reinforcers of children's behaviours as star charts and smiley faces, and approaches such as time out and the 'naughty step' that are used to discourage and extinguish behaviours they feel to be undesirable.

STRENGTHS AND WEAKNESSES OF THE THEORY

The principles of behaviourism have been applied in classrooms and early years settings for many years and have provided an effective means of changing many children's behaviours for the better. Critics have, however, drawn attention to the idea that behaviourism has fallen short of engaging with the complex nature of children's thinking, the part that motivation plays in children's learning and the impact of social and cultural contexts on learning. The theory has also been criticized on the grounds that it fails to take into account inherited factors. Behaviourism is, in many respects, different to most other theories of learning. In essence, it focuses more on behaviour than on the holistic nature of childhood and learning. It has been criticized on the grounds that it pays only limited regard to children's emotions.

Children's learning from their first days is reinforced through all manner of external stimuli

view the YouTube video, 'Behaviorism: Pavlov, Watson, and Skinner': www.youtube.com/watch?v=xvVaTy8mQrg, which explores differences between the ideas of three key theorists in the field of behaviourism. Now view the following, 'Teaching and Learning Approaches: Behaviorism, Cognitivism and Social Constructivism': www.youtube.com/watch?v=gkzLAz25KPI, which explores differences between behaviourism and the ideas of Piaget and Vygotsky.

ACTIVITIES AND POINTS FOR DISCUSSION

Activity: Take time to locate and view the behaviour policy of an early years setting that you are familiar with. What are the key aims of the policy? Identify any positive reinforcers within the policy that adults might implement in order to shape children's behaviours.

Discussion Point: Having completed the activity above, discuss why some behaviour policies in early years settings and primary schools are more effective than others. How might a better understanding of the principles of operant conditioning improve outcomes for shaping children's behaviours?

LINKS TO OTHER THEORIES

Behaviourism contrasts markedly with most other theories of learning and child development as it focuses primarily on behaviour, with relatively little attention being paid to those inner processes that take place within the brain and that we generally conceive of as 'thinking' or 'cognition'. Unlike the theories of Piaget and Freud, behaviourism is not a stage-based theory and does not view children as passing through stages of development. Take time to

EXTENDED AND RECOMMENDED READING

McLeod, S.A. (2015) Skinner: Operant Conditioning. Available at: www.simplypsychology.org/operant-conditioning.html (accessed 06.11.17).

Wheldall, K. (2012) *The Behaviourist in the Classroom*. Oxford: Routledge.

REFERENCES

Gray, C. and MacBlain, S.F. (2015) *Learning Theories in Childhood*. London: Sage.

MacBlain, S.F. (2014) *How Children Learn*. London: Sage.

Watson, J.B. (1928) *Psychological Care of Infant and Child*. New York: Norton.

JEAN PIAGET: AN ENDURING LEGACY

THE THEORIST (1896–1980)

Jean Piaget was born in Neuchâtel in Switzerland, achieving a doctorate in Natural Sciences in 1918. In 1929, he became Professor of Child Psychology at the University of Geneva. Piaget became aware early on that mistakes in learning made by young children were consistently different to those made by older children; he accounted for this by arguing that thinking, or more specifically cognitive processing, in younger children is essentially different to that in older children and adults. This led him to develop a theory which could explain thinking in children. He, therefore, proposed that children and adults demonstrate typical patterns of thinking and learning at different stages of their lives.

KEY PUBLICATIONS

Piaget, J. (1926/2002) *The Language and Thought of the Child*. London: Routledge Classics. [Originally published in French in 1926]

Piaget, J. (1947/2001) *The Psychology of Intelligence*. London: Routledge Classics. [Originally published in French in 1947]

Patterns of behaviour are learned through experiences created by adults

UNDERSTANDING THE THEORY

SCHEMA

Piaget believed that when young children are presented with new information they may not immediately understand it unless they have already constructed within their own thinking relevant knowledge and understanding, which they have gained from interacting with the environments in which they are growing up. It is through interacting with their environments that children from their earliest years begin to build internal mental representations in their brains, which Piaget referred to as *schema*. Cathy Nutbrown (2006, p. 7) has explained *schema* as 'a way of labelling children's consistent patterns of action'. Nutbrown went further

and indicated how practitioners can observe schema or patterns of children's behaviours taking place. Through observing schema or patterns in children's behaviours, practitioners can then become much more informed about how to create situations in which children learn more effectively and with more purpose.

ASSIMILATION AND ACCOMMODATION

In attempting to understand schema, it is also important to differentiate these from *concepts*. Hayes (1994, pp. 143–4) has referred to schema as being like cognitive maps, which enable such activities as planning whilst concepts are to do with classifying objects and phenomena. Hayes also emphasized how Piaget had placed great emphasis on children acting on their environments, which are at the heart of children's thinking. By acting on their environments, children *assimilate* and then *accommodate* new information, which then guides their behaviours and learning. *Assimilation* is where new information comes to be absorbed by the child within their *schema* without any real manipulation of that information. *Accommodation* is where *schema* then develop, in order to facilitate the acquisition of the new information.

View the YouTube video, 'Schemas, assimilation, and accommodation': www.youtube.com/watch?v=BMc9TPwoVxQ, which explores 'schemas', 'assimilation' and 'accommodation' and how these processes contribute to what Piaget referred to as 'equilibrium'.

STAGES OF INTELLECTUAL DEVELOPMENT

Further to his ideas on *schema*, Piaget argued that cognitive development in children follows a series of stages, which he suggested are 'invariant', that is, they pass through one stage before progressing to the next. Piaget's stages are as follows:

THE SENSORIMOTOR STAGE (0–2 YEARS)

Piaget saw the first stage of cognitive growth as the *sensorimotor stage*. This is when infants learn through their senses. They do this through, for example, sucking, touching, and visually attending to others around them. Piaget suggested that newly born infants are not capable of 'thinking', but instead engage in a whole range of reflexive activities such as grasping, which are essentially innate and which they are born with.

THE PREOPERATIONAL STAGE (2–7 YEARS)

Language is a key feature of this next stage as it is language that greatly facilitates the development of *schema* through *assimilation* and *accommodation*. This stage involves two further sub-stages – the

Experience of the environment builds intellectual development and promotes learning

Learning through imitation is a powerful means of developing thinking *preconceptual* (2–4 years) and the *intuitive* (4–7 years). During the first of these, children increasingly engage in imaginative and symbolic play which typically involves an increasing use of words and symbols to represent objects or people. Imitation of the behaviours of others can be observed during this stage. Piaget saw play as an essential element in the cognitive development of young children at this stage. He acknowledged, however, that children's thinking during this stage can be limited by such factors as 'egocentrism', 'rigidity in thinking' and 'transductive reasoning' (MacBlain, 2014). 'Egocentrism' seeks to explain why young children appear unable to see the world from the perspective of others. With 'rigidity in thinking', Piaget believed that children of this age have not developed to a level whereby they can reverse sequences and adapt meaningfully to a change in the appearance of their immediate environment. 'Transductive reasoning'

can be observed where young children make inferences about relationships when, in reality, there are none. Such thinking begins to disappear around the age of 4 years. Thinking, however, in the latter stage of the preoperational stage appears to remain intuitive, i.e. it is based on such observables as shape, size and colour, as opposed to being logical (MacBlain, 2014).

Piaget believed that during the *intuitive stage* (4–7 years) children are developing their thinking to levels where they can start to stand back and see the whole, as opposed to previously being only able to see the details of things. He referred to this process as *decentring* and suggested that children's thinking also remains limited here, in as much as they have not yet fully developed the capacity to shift attention away from the detail of something and transfer it to the whole and back again. A child at this stage, for example, who is observing an adult pouring a fixed amount of water from a short fat glass into a long slim glass, will typically say that there is more water in the taller glass. Piaget referred to this type of thinking as *conservation* and proposed that a child's capacity to conserve marks the ending of the preoperational stage and the beginning of the next stage, concrete operations.

CONCRETE OPERATIONAL STAGE (7–11 YEARS)

A key difference between the preoperational stage and the concrete operational stage is that, in the latter, children have now developed the capacity to apply logic as a way of problem solving. Piaget proposed that logic, which is characterized by operational rules, develops gradually, as children construct newer and more

Thinking needs to be supported by careful observation and purposeful activity

Exploring the natural world builds capacity for logical thinking and future problem solving

complicated skills and organize these into increasingly complex semantic structures. In this way, children's thinking becomes more flexible, though it remains constrained by the need to have concrete objects present. Piaget used the term 'horizontal decalage' to explain the inconsistencies in development which can be observed in children. This can be better understood in terms of the inconsistent performance by children when engaged in tasks that require them to process similar mental operations. Whilst some children will readily succeed with certain tasks, other children of the same age will not.

FORMAL OPERATIONAL STAGE (11–15 YEARS)

It is during this stage, Piaget argued, that children's cognitive development can be observed at its highest level. Thinking at this stage is more flexible and more symbolic and is no longer limited to the experience of the child, or their immediate reality. Children can, for example, start to think and talk with others about the future and can transcend themselves to other places and situations using language. Experiences can also be dealt with in a more objective way. Piaget further argued that during this stage thinking becomes more logical, with children being observed engaging in deductive reasoning. Children begin to test hypotheses and to be more objective and reflective in their thinking.

WHAT THE THEORY LOOKS LIKE IN PRACTICE

Piaget argued that teachers need to engage children in tasks that are stimulating and that are appropriate to their stage of development, as opposed to trying to accelerate their learning. Though this view gained acceptance at the time, it also generated considerable debate and, in some quarters, was heavily criticized, particularly by those who viewed children's cognitive development as uneven across the general population. Whilst Piaget initially believed that teaching should be appropriate to the age of the child, he later altered this view, acknowledging that children's thinking develops at different rates and, therefore, they may be capable of engaging in more sophisticated and intellectually challenging learning. This is an important point, for during the 1960s and 1970s much practice in the UK was informed by Piaget's early views that children might not have developed their thinking enough to progress to more challenging elements of learning.

Piaget was not just interested in how children arrive at correct answers to problems, but also why they failed to arrive at the correct answers. This has become an important aspect of practice in early years education and primary schools where practitioners and teachers are encouraged to understand children's misconceptions and why they may repeat errors.

Experiences provided by adults prepare the way for intellectual development and future learning

CASE STUDY: EGOCENTRISM IN ACTION

Jane is 2 years of age and is playing the game 'hide and seek'. To her older brother's frustration, on each occasion that they play the game she turns around and covers her eyes. She thinks that because she cannot see her brother and her eyes are closed, he is unable to see her. Piaget believed that this kind of thinking, which he referred to as *egocentrism*, pervades the thinking of children at this age. He also suggested that it went some way to offering an explanation as to why young children can be observed to ascribe feelings to objects around them.

CASE STUDY: RIGIDITY IN THINKING

Martin's dad is looking after him whilst his wife is visiting relatives. He begins to prepare lunch and cooks four sausages and some vegetables. He then sits Martin in his highchair and places two sausages in Martin's bowl and two on his own plate. On reflection, he reconsiders the number of sausages he has given himself as he is quite hungry. He quickly reaches over and takes back one of Martin's sausages for himself. On seeing this, Martin goes into spasms of anger because he has had one of his sausages taken from him – now there is only one sausage in his bowl. Martin's dad, however, who has recently studied the work of Piaget, promptly cuts Martin's one remaining sausage into lots of smaller pieces – Martin looks at his bowl, which now has 'lots of sausages' in it, and immediately stops crying and starts to eat – he now appears happy because he 'thinks' he has 'lots of sausages'.

CASE STUDY: TRANSDUCTIVE REASONING IN ACTION

Young children make inferences about relationships where there may be none. Take Oliver, for example, whose mother is pregnant with his sister-to-be. He observes his mother to have a very large tummy and when he sees other women who are overweight, he asks his mother if they will also be having a baby. Here, Oliver is relying only on what he observes, that is size, as opposed to applying logic.

Importantly, Piaget focused on the idea of *readiness* and the notion that instead of children being accelerated in their learning, they should be viewed as being at certain *stages* of *readiness* before being progressed, by their teachers, on to approaching tasks and problems that are more intellectually demanding.

STRENGTHS AND WEAKNESSES OF THE THEORY

Piaget has been criticized on the grounds that he saw cognitive development as being defined by different stages, in contrast, for example, to the thinking of Vygotsky and Bruner. Later on, Piaget (1970) modified this view, as with other aspects of his theory, to suggest more of a 'spiral' process of intellectual development in children, reflecting an expanding and upward process through which children actively engage in reconstructing existing knowledge. He did not, however, account for why

children are driven to move from one stage to another. Methods used by Piaget to investigate how children learn have been criticized as the sample sizes were small, the language used in his experimental situations was at times too complex for the children (Meadows, 1993) and he tended to observe his own children.

Donaldson (1978) was especially critical of the sort of questions Piaget used in his experiments with children, suggesting that these were too often asked in a manner as to 'catch children out' rather than help them. Piaget was also accused of generalizing observations which were taken from white, middle-class children of largely educated parents. Donaldson (1978) cautioned that Piaget had suggested how children were limited by the stage of development they were at when, in fact, his perceived limitations of children's thinking and development were more to do with the nature of the tasks he set the children. Donaldson's ideas, related in her celebrated text *Children's Minds*, are worth considering as they offer excellent insights into the potential shortcomings of Piaget's ideas.

LINKS TO OTHER THEORIES

Piaget believed that knowledge and meaning are actively constructed by children through interacting with the environments in which they live and grow up. Such a belief can be seen as a major departure from the ideas of the behaviourists who viewed children's learning and development as more of a passive state where children are, in effect, the recipients of information that arises from the environments in which they live (MacBlain, 2014). Piaget's ideas were well received at the time and grew in popularity, influencing the practice of many early years practitioners and primary teachers for decades. Indeed, his ideas continue to influence much thinking practice in the early years even today. Piaget also departed from the emphasis that behaviourists had placed on undertaking 'artificial' experiments with children in laboratory settings, choosing instead to observe and listen carefully to children as they engaged in natural activities and in natural settings. In contrast to the behaviourists, Piaget very much led the way in exploring and accounting for those internal processes that underpin learning and explain thinking. He gave to researchers in the field of education and psychology new ways of explaining early child development, most notably observation with an important emphasis on child-centredness and language.

For Piaget, it was the 'whole' child that should be at the centre of experimentation and not just the observable behaviours. Those who embraced the ideas of Piaget and, particularly, early years practitioners have also been drawn to the similarities between his ideas and those of other theorists such as Froebel, Montessori and Dewey, especially the view that young children learn best when engaged in practical activities where the role of teachers and practitioners is to nurture children's social and emotional development by removing any artificial barriers to learning (MacBlain and Bowman, 2016). Like Dewey, Piaget viewed the role of the teacher/practitioner very much in terms of child-centredness and dependent to a large extent on the environment. The child was to be viewed in terms of engaging in 'discovery' and this was to be at the very centre of learning.

ACTIVITIES AND POINTS FOR DISCUSSION

Activity: Identify activities that you have observed children engaging in that might indicate increased cognitive development. Then, consider what role language might have played in this process.

Discussion Point: Do children develop through identifiable stages? If so, what is your evidence for believing this and, if not, offer a rationale to support your own views?

EXTENDED AND RECOMMENDED READING

Athey, C. (1990/2003) *Extending Thought in Young Children: A Parent–Teacher Partnership*. London: Paul Chapman Publishing/Sage.

Gray, C. and MacBlain, S.F. (2015) *Learning Theories in Childhood* (2nd edn). London: Sage.

Nutbrown, C. (2006) *Threads of Thinking: Young Children Learning and the Role of Early Education*. London: Sage.

REFERENCES

Donaldson, M. (1978) *Children's Minds*. Glasgow: Collins, Fontana.

Hayes, N. (1994) *Foundations of Psychology*. London: Routledge.

MacBlain, S.F. (2014) *How Children Learn*. London: Sage.

MacBlain, S.F. and Bowman, H. (2016) 'Teaching and learning', in D. Wyse and S. Rogers (eds), *A Guide to Early Years and Primary Teaching*. London: Sage.

Meadows, S. (1993) *The Child as Thinker: The Development and Acquisition of Cognition in Childhood*. London: Routledge.

Nutbrown, C. (2006) *Threads of Thinking: Young Children Learning and the Role of Early Education*. London: Sage.

Piaget, J. (1970) *Science of Education and the Psychology of the Child*. New York: Orion.

LEV VYGOTSKY: LEARNING AND SOCIAL CONSTRUCTIVISM

THE THEORIST (1896–1934)

Lev Vygotsky was born into a society that would see significant and, in some respects, catastrophic change during his lifetime. Born in Belarus, then part of Russia, to a Jewish family, he lived through the Russian revolution, the execution of the Russian Czar and his family, World War I and much of the Soviet era under Stalin, in which many of his countrymen were punished, executed or sent to labour camps in Siberia. Vygotsky studied at the prestigious Moscow University and as a child was considered intellectually very able. He became a prolific writer and was much influenced by the ideas of Freud and Piaget. Vygotsky had a particular interest in the potential relevance of psychology to education. It is perhaps an understatement to say that many of his ideas have come to influence thinking and practice in the field of educational psychology today. Sadly, Vygotsky died early, during his thirties.

KEY PUBLICATION

Vygotsky, L. (1978) *Mind in Society* (ed. M. Cole et al.). Cambridge, MA: Harvard University Press.

UNDERSTANDING THE THEORY

To fully understand Vygotsky's theory and his ideas on education and child development, it is necessary to understand the society in which he lived. At the time, Russia was in turmoil with different factions fighting each other and communism emerging as the basis for the future USSR in which Vygotsky then lived, under the leadership of Lenin and later Stalin. Russia or, as it became known, the USSR was then very different to Western European countries. Communism was the dominant political ideology of the time and those who opposed government directives or the communist ideology could be punished severely. Vygotsky, therefore, formulated his thinking within what many in the West would have viewed as a closed and overly oppressive society where thinking was greatly restricted and subjected to censure, often resulting in severe penalties. Education during this time was heavily controlled by the state. There can be little doubt that Vygotsky's ideas on children's education and learning were heavily influenced by this society and by the government ideologies of communism.

Vygotsky saw all learning as being founded on 'experiential learning' with much of children's learning occurring prior to formal education. Whitebread (2012, p. 127) has very cleverly encapsulated this central feature of Vygotsky's theory as follows:

> [A]ll learning begins in the social context, which supports children in the processes whereby they construct their own understandings ... all learning exists first at the 'inter-mental' level in the form of spoken language, and then at the 'intramental' level (i.e. within the child's mind, in the form of internal language, or thought) ... This has been termed the 'social constructivist' approach to learning.

Students who study the work of Vygotsky and those who have written about him quickly come across references to the 'Zone of Proximal Development' (ZPD), which, arguably, has become overly representative of his work to the exclusion of many of his other ideas (MacBlain, 2014). Whilst this notion of ZPD is at the core of Vygotsky's theory, it also needs to be understood that this term really only appeared on a very few of the literally thousands of pages written by Vygotsky. ZPD was defined by Vygotsky (1978, p. 86), cited in Gray and MacBlain (2015, p. 99) as:

> those functions which have yet to mature but are in the process of maturing ...'buds' or 'flowers' of development rather than 'fruits' of development. The actual development level characterizes the cognitive development retrospectively, whilst the ZPD characterizes it prospectively.

SOCIAL CONSTRUCTIVISM

Vygotsky introduced us to the idea of *social constructivism*, where particular emphasis is placed on the cultures that children are born into and their social environments as a means of trying to understand how they construct their knowledge. This is not surprising given the impositions placed on Vygotsky by the culture and society in which he lived. Vygotsky saw culture as those social patterns of behaviour and beliefs that are passed on to children throughout the generations. In practice, culture, he suggested, becomes passed on to children through the use of such 'tools' as nursery rhymes, art and children's stories. Today, cultural tools have become far more sophisticated and now include social media, digital technology, television, and so on. Vygotsky proposed that cultural tools play a crucial role in the development of children's thinking and learning. Pea (1993, p. 52) commented some decades ago on cultural tools, as follows: 'these tools literally carry intelligence in them, in that they represent some individual's or some community's decision that the means thus offered would be reified, made stable as quasi permanent, for the use of others.'

It is now generally accepted (Gray and MacBlain, 2015; MacBlain, 2014) that cultural tools influence children's perception of others and the events they experience, as well as the world in which they grow up. One only needs to reflect on the cultural tools in society today, such as children's TV programmes, social media sites, movie and pop stars, to appreciate the powerful influence of culture on children's learning and social development.

Vygotsky saw the most important cultural tool in children's learning to be language. He believed that through talking and listening, children come to develop their abilities to understand and comprehend events and the world around them. The high level of importance given by Vygotsky to language in developing children's thinking and learning was highlighted just over a decade ago, as follows: 'Speech does not merely serve as the expression of developed thought. Thought is restructured as it is transformed into speech' (Vygotsky, 1987, cited in Holzman, 2006, p. 115). For Vygotsky, language is the means by which meaning can be transmitted to children. By using language, children engage with those around them and, by doing so, engage in a process whereby they become active members of the communities in which they grow up as well as society at large. It is the reciprocal nature of this social engagement with others that lies at the heart of Vygotsky's 'social constructivism'.

Vygotsky also believed that children are born with the foundations for thinking, for example attention, memory and visual recognition, which will then enable their development of higher order thinking. He proposed that children develop higher order thinking skills and abilities in order to engage in solving problems, reasoning and recalling memory (Rose et al., 2003). Vygotsky also suggested that children are born with the ability to learn through guidance from others, such as parents, siblings and significant others. In this way, the cultural norms of their communities and wider society are passed on and developed within the child. Vygotsky (1978, p. 57) commented, for example, on how 'every function in the child's cultural development appears twice: first, on the social level, and later on the individual level; first, between people ... and then inside the child'.

Vygotsky also emphasized an important distinction between lower and higher order thinking, suggesting that the former was characterized by biological functions such as memory and attention, and the latter by such functions as problem solving, logical reasoning and intentionality. He proposed that the social activities children engage in can be understood in terms of a bridge which children cross as a means of moving from lower to higher order thinking.

STAGES OR INCREMENTS

At the core of Vygotsky's theory lies four stages; Vygotsky's idea of stages was very different to that of Piaget. Vygotsky was not proposing a fixed stage approach as Piaget had done. Gray and MacBlain (2015, p. 98) have explained this as follows:

> Unlike Piaget, Vygotsky did not advocate a staged unidirectional approach to development ... he believed that development is progressive and tends to follow an incremental pathway ... he acknowledged that a child may move backwards or forwards between stages ... as their thoughts mature. Problem novelty or difficulty can cause a child to regress to an earlier stage, whereas experience will progress development.

Gray and MacBlain (2015, p. 97) went on to describe Vygotsky's idea of stages thus:

> **Primitive stage**: Children under 2 years of age use vocal activity as a means of emotional expression and for social engagement ... behaviour becomes increasingly purposeful and goal-directed ... thought and language are separate.

Practical intelligence: During this stage, the child's language uses syntactic (rules of speech) and logical forms. These forms of speech are linked to the child's practical problem-solving activities.

External symbolic stage: Thinking aloud is common ... with language used to help with internal problem solving ... Thinking aloud enables the child to self-regulate and plan their activities.

Internalization of symbolic tools: Between 7 and 8 years of age, children internalize thinking ... Problem solving continues to be guided by speech but the voice is internal ... This stage leads to greater cognitive independence, flexibility and freedom.

Children are born with the ability to learn through guidance from others, for example their parents and grandparents

WHAT THE THEORY LOOKS LIKE IN PRACTICE

To aid our understanding of Vygotsky's theory, it is useful to focus on play, which is key to children's early learning. Vygotsky saw play as central to children's learning and emphasized how it is through play that children progress their understanding of relationships. Vygotsky viewed play in terms of 'self-education' and not simply as activities that are repeated. For Vygotsky, play was an active process often characterized by the mimicking of others but also, more importantly, by a growth in independence. Through early play, children increasingly develop the ability to play by themselves, to be autonomous and to take risks. As their confidence grows, children increasingly take more control over their play and internalize self-made rules as well as learning how to accept rules made by others. Fantasy emerges as a key feature of children's play. In summary, Vygotsky viewed children's play as being essentially spontaneous and self-initiated and as part of a naturally developing process of self-regulation. He proposed that through play and other social activities, children create their own ZPD by setting personal levels of challenge; they also learn to set their own personal levels of control (Whitebread, 2012). In this way, the play and activities they choose to engage in become appropriate to their actual stage of development.

View the YouTube video, 'Scaffolding Language Skills': www.youtube.com/watch?v=12TcwDSrdnM, which offers an excellent example of scaffolding in the classroom.

CASE STUDY: LEARNING THROUGH GUIDANCE FROM ADULTS

Albie is 5 years of age and was assessed recently at his primary school by an educational psychologist. Albie's parents were given a report by the psychologist, which indicated how Albie had a verbal IQ of 75 and a non-verbal IQ of 80 (average range: 85–115). Some months after the assessment, Albie changed schools; his parents gave a copy of the psychologist's report to his new teacher, which stated that Albie was of low general ability and would be best suited to working in a low set. Following his move, however, Albie blossomed. His new teacher spent much time with Albie, teaching him new strategies for approaching tasks and providing many opportunities for him to gain in self-confidence, and especially to develop his vocabulary and general language abilities with encouragement to read widely and often. Albie gradually grew in his love of reading and gained greatly in confidence. When Albie moved school, his new teacher worked with him in a way that showed she believed he was more capable than had been reported by his previous school. His teacher taught him new strategies to develop his learning, new ways to approach and think about problems, and focused on increasing his vocabulary and general language and raising his self-esteem. His teacher also encouraged group-based activities where the children worked with Albie in groups to solve problems, learn from one another and construct new understandings. The latter school's philosophy of learning was very much in keeping with that of Vygotsky. Albie's new teacher was purposefully structuring the classroom environment in small ways to progress Albie's thinking and to support him in moving towards becoming a more independent learner. The teacher recognized the importance of developing his language and did this through a range of devices, such as listening attentively to Albie, asking focused and purposeful questions, and understanding that the questioning had a real and valuable purpose, which was to develop Albie's thinking.

CASE STUDY: USING LANGUAGE TO DEVELOP THINKING

Ryan has started attending a local playgroup and comes from a family where television dominates family activity. For most of his time at home, Ryan can be observed to be watching television. Mealtimes are generally chaotic with meals being eaten on trays whilst the family watch television. Ryan's language is quite delayed and is characterized by an impoverished vocabulary, few attempts at initiating conversation with others, immature speech and a lack of confidence when it comes to engaging in social activities with his peers.

The head of Ryan's playgroup discusses Ryan's levels of intellectual development with her staff and initiates a programme for Ryan, which has at its core a focus on extending his vocabulary through naming games and activities with an adult, and playing collaboratively with peers on exciting and rewarding problem-solving tasks where good language structures are modelled to Ryan by his more articulate and verbally competent peers. As the days progress, it becomes apparent that Ryan is now using more complicated language structures, new words in sentences and, importantly, is initiating and taking the lead in conversation with others. His level and quality of social interaction are progressing extremely well, leading to a growing interest in books and reading.

STRENGTHS AND WEAKNESSES OF THE THEORY

For Vygotsky, the nature of learning may be dissimilar in different cultures. This differs from Piaget who would have argued that cognitive development is universal across different cultures. Like Bruner, Vygotsky believed that children's cognitive development arises from their social interactions and through supported learning from others that encourage the construction of knowledge. By contrast, Piaget believed that children's cognitive development arises essentially through their own explorations of the environments in which they live and grow up. Vygotsky placed much greater emphasis on the importance of language than Piaget, which has been a key criticism of Piaget's theory. When Vygotsky's work was translated into English, it often contained inaccuracies.

LINKS TO OTHER THEORIES

Unlike other theorists such as Piaget and Bruner and the early philosophers, Vygotsky did not focus on children's learning as being age-related and did not

properly create and develop a theory of children's development. Schaffer (2004, p. 201) has, for example, commented on how the only pronouncement Vygotsky made regarding age was to propose that 'children up to 2 years are influenced primarily by biological forces and that the socio-cultural influences ... do not come into play until after that age'.

Vygotsky was in fact less interested in the individual nature of learning in children and more so in the cultural contexts within which children grow up. In this respect, the focus of his theory was like that of Bronfenbrenner, who focused more on the social, political, economic and cultural contexts within which children grow up. This may not be surprising in view of the fact that he lived in a Marxist state where, it can be argued, individualism was less encouraged than the collective, which was largely dominated by the government of his time. Vygotsky saw children's development and learning less in terms of an individual process and more as the sum of the relationships they develop with others, with whom they have come into contact. Like Bronfenbrenner, he emphasized how children do not grow up in isolation but within social matrices that are created by and maintained through the dynamic nature of those relationships they have with others. According to Wertsch (1981, p. 164), cited in Gray and MacBlain (2015, p. 93), 'it is through others that we develop into ourselves'.

Vygotsky placed much greater emphasis than Piaget on the important role that culture plays in developing children's thinking and learning and did not give the same emphasis as Piaget to stages of development.

ACTIVITIES AND POINTS FOR DISCUSSION

Activity: Create a checklist of ways in which practitioners might assess the impact that children's cultures have on their learning. Having done so, prioritize these from the most important to the least important, with a clear rationale as to your choices.

Discussion Point: Why might all types of language in the home be considered important for children's social and cognitive development?

EXTENDED AND RECOMMENDED READING

Daniels, H. (ed.) (2005) *An Introduction to Vygotsky* (2nd edn). London: Taylor & Francis. (An accessible and informative account of Vygotsky's ideas.)

Whitebread, D. (2012) *Developmental Psychology and Early Childhood Education*. London: Sage. (A comprehensive and readable text that contextualizes theoretical accounts of child development in early years practice.)

REFERENCES

Gray, C. and MacBlain, S.F. (2015) *Learning Theories in Childhood* (2nd edn). London: Sage.

Holzman, L. (2006) 'Activating postmodernism', *Theory and Psychology*, 16(1): 109–23.

MacBlain, S.F. (2014) *How Children Learn*. London: Sage.

Pea, R.D. (1993) 'Practices of distributed intelligence and designs for education', in G. Salomon (ed.), *Distributed Cognitions* (pp. 47–87). New York: Cambridge University Press.

Rose, S.A., Feldman, J.F. and Jankowski, J.J. (2003) 'The building blocks of cognition', *The Journal of Pediatrics*, 143(4): 54–61.

Schaffer, H.R. (2004) *Introducing Child Psychology*. Oxford: Blackwell.

Vygotsky, L.S. (1978) *Mind in Society: The Development of Higher Psychological Processes*. Cambridge, MA: Harvard University Press.

Whitebread, D. (2012) *Developmental Psychology and Early Childhood Education*. London: Sage.

ALBERT BANDURA AND SOCIAL LEARNING THEORY

THE THEORIST (1925 – PRESENT)

Albert Bandura was born in Alberta, Canada and, like other theorists who went before him, he challenged the thinking of his time regarding education and learning. In so doing, he offered a significant shift in how we might understand children's learning and early development. Bandura is perhaps best known for his 'social learning theory'; in 1986, he changed the name of his theory to 'social cognitive theory', to reflect what he saw as the far greater and more complex nature of children's thinking and how they learned.

KEY PUBLICATIONS

Bandura, A. (1977) *Social Learning Theory*. Englewood Cliffs, NJ: Prentice Hall.

Bandura, A. (1997) *Self-efficacy: The Exercise of Control*. New York: Freeman.

UNDERSTANDING THE THEORY

Bandura saw social factors as being key to our understanding of how children learn (Bandura, 1977). He believed that children's learning does not always encompass changes in behaviour and that children might observe others without these observations (*stimuli*) resulting in changes in their own behaviours (*response*). He also firmly believed that motivation was central to children's learning and that children's levels of motivation could in fact influence the way in which they observed the behaviours of others, thus contributing to their own learning.

THE BOBO DOLL EXPERIMENT

Bandura is often associated with his 'Bobo doll' experiment in the early 1960s, in which he filmed a woman aggressively hitting a large toy doll. Bandura invited a group of young children to view the film and then asked them to play in a separate room where there was a similar doll. The children started hitting the doll as they had observed the woman doing in the film. They were, in effect, imitating the woman's actions. Of significance was the fact that the children hit the doll even though they were not being rewarded for doing so. They were, in practice, engaging in the behaviours they had observed but that had not been reinforced in any way by, for example, receiving a reward. Bandura argued, therefore, that learning was taking place because of observation and not because of reinforcement, as behaviourists at the time would have argued. This idea, then, challenged some of the key principles of 'behaviourist' theory.

IMITATION AND IDENTIFICATION

Bandura proposed two key elements central to children's learning – *imitation* and *identification*. Children, he argued, imitate the actions of those around them and, through identifying with others, assimilate new learning into already existing concepts. Through this process, fresh patterns of behaviour become internalized within children's

By identifying with the actions of others, children increase their potential for social learning

cognitive structures, with the result that they then act in a manner they believe adults will act. Bandura emphasized that for meaningful and purposeful learning to take place, the behaviours of those being imitated should be appropriate. He also drew attention to symbolic modelling where children imitate and identify with fictional characters, for example those found in fairy tales and children's stories. Readers will also be familiar with the way in which children imitate characters they have seen on television.

SELF-EFFICACY

A further key element in Bandura's theory is the idea of 'self-efficacy' (Bandura, 1997), which he saw as a child's belief in their ability to do well and succeed in different situations, and their capacity to exercise control over their own actions. Bandura emphasized how self-efficacy is strongly related to children's thinking and actions and, importantly, their emotional state. Children with poor self-efficacy, he proposed, can be observed to avoid tasks that present a challenge, preferring instead to focus on the negative (MacBlain and Gray, 2016). They can be observed to engage in framing their thoughts within patterns of thinking that have been internalized over previous years and through which they come to persuade themselves that they will not be successful. Children with poor self-efficacy often present as having poor self-confidence and low self-esteem and typically do less well than those with strong self-efficacy. They may demonstrate less interest in attempting tasks and seeing these through to completion. They may also demonstrate more anxiety than their peers when asked to engage in problem-based learning tasks.

Colverd and Hodgkin (2011, p. 36) have emphasized how these children can internalize limitations on what they think is possible and may even believe that certain tasks are beyond their abilities when in actual fact they are not. This lack of belief in their own abilities can, in turn, affect their motivation and ultimately their commitment to learning: 'I can't do this, it's boring' signals 'I don't believe I can be successful with this and therefore I don't want to take the risk'. Importantly, Bandura suggested that a significant element in the acquisition of strong self-efficacy in children is their development of 'mastery' through experiences. He suggested that children do this by, for example, observing others around them who are successful, receiving positive affirmation from adults and peers and, importantly, learning to understand and manage their own emotions and feelings.

WHAT THE THEORY LOOKS LIKE IN PRACTICE

It is possible to observe the principles that underpin Bandura's theory in everyday practice where young children are learning. Imitating the actions of others is commonplace and young children frequently identify with older children, adults, and characters they have watched on TV, film and the internet, or come across in story books.

STRENGTHS AND WEAKNESSES OF THE THEORY

A major strength of Bandura's theory was that it challenged the thinking and practice of the time, which was largely influenced by the legacies of Freud

CASE STUDY: DEVELOPING SELF-EFFICACY

Sophie is in her first year working at a nursery school in a socially disadvantaged area. She identifies four children whom she observes regularly hold back from attempting activities set by the adults. She watches how they withdraw from activities without even attempting them, preferring to engage in activities that are familiar to them. Sophie meets at the end of the day with the other adults and they decide to devise structured activities for these four children and, initially, to invite them to attempt the activities. If they hold back, they will then model to the children how to attempt the activities and then invite the children to have a go. When the children then attempt the activities, the staff will give lots of encouragement and praise, especially if they complete the activities. Importantly, the staff then sit with the children after they have successfully completed the activities and explain to them in clear and simple ways why they have been able to succeed and what behaviours they used to achieve success. After some weeks, Sophie starts to observe how the children appear more confident with attempting new activities and look to the adults for support and encouragement.

CASE STUDY: NEW LEARNING THROUGH IMITATION

Jasmine has been working in a local playgroup for over ten years and has recently had a new child named Dwayne join her group. Reports written about the new child emphasize that he is 'very shy' and 'finds difficulty making friends and managing relationships'. Jasmine recognizes that Dwayne lacks confidence and, though he is very young, has poor self-efficacy. She decides to arrange activities where Dwayne plays and works with two other boys, Khamil and Freddie, who are very confident and who have been assessed as being intellectually very able. She observes over the coming weeks how Dwayne increasingly imitates the other children and how they take time to support Dwayne and show him how to do those things that they find easy but he finds difficult. After a few months, Dwayne's confidence in his own abilities appears to have increased greatly; his language is much improved and he appears to have adopted some of the behaviour patterns of Khamil and Freddie.

and the behaviourists. Bandura drew attention to the importance of the social environment for children's learning and the impact significant others have in modelling learning to children. Whilst Bandura's theory has numerous strengths and can account for many aspects of children's behaviour, it has been criticized for not going far enough in explaining, for example, how children acquire and develop inner thoughts and feelings; it is now accepted that even from an early age, most children's cognitive capacity has developed to such an extent that they are potentially able to exert control over their emotions. It is also recognized that most children from an early age can resist imitating the behaviours of others and can also resist identifying with different types of role modelling (MacBlain, 2014).

ACTIVITIES AND POINTS FOR DISCUSSION

Activity: Take time to view the following link: McLeod, S.A. (2011, updated 2014) Bobo Doll Experiment. Available at: www.simplypsychology.org/bobo-doll.html, and identify what you consider to be the ethical issues surrounding such an experiment.

Discussion Point: Having viewed the above link and identified key ethical issues, design a situation or series of activities in which you might ethically research aggression in children. Consider the extent to which you would have to take into account any differences in learning between boys and girls.

LINKS TO OTHER THEORIES

At the heart of Bandura's theory was his emphasis on the need to recognize children's feelings and emotions and how these impact on learning. In this respect, his ideas are very similar to those of Bruner and Vygotsky and early philosophers and thinkers such as Pestalozzi, Steiner and Montessori. Bandura's ideas, however, contrast markedly with those of the early behaviourists who focused almost entirely on the links between *stimuli* and *response*, which bring about changes in children's behaviours. Bandura argued that this focus on 'stimulus–response' learning was far too simplistic and failed to go far enough in explaining the complexity of children's behaviour and learning, especially their feelings and emotions.

EXTENDED AND RECOMMENDED READING

Bandura, A., Ross, D. and Ross, S.A. (1961) 'Transmission of aggression through the imitation of aggressive models', *Journal of Abnormal and Social Psychology*, 63: 575–82.

MacBlain, S.F. and Gray, C. (2016) 'Pioneers: Bandura and Bronfenbrenner explained', *Early Educator*, 18(1): 38–44.

REFERENCES

Bandura, A. (1977) *Social Learning Theory*. Englewood Cliffs, NJ: Prentice Hall.

Bandura, A. (1997) *Self-efficacy: The Exercise of Control*. New York: Freeman.

Colverd, S. and Hodgkin, B. (2011) *Developing Emotional Intelligence in the Primary School*. London: Routledge.

MacBlain, S.F. (2014) *How Children Learn*. London: Sage.

MacBlain, S.F. and Gray, C. (2016) 'Pioneers: Bandura and Bronfenbrenner explained', *Early Educator*, 18(1): 38–44.

URIE BRONFENBRENNER: LEARNING IN THE WIDER CONTEXT

THE THEORIST (1917–2005)

Bronfenbrenner was born in Moscow and at 6 years of age moved to the USA. In 1979, he published a seminal text, *The Ecology of Human Development*, where he set out his views on child development. Bronfenbrenner was a co-founder of the Head Start programme and is perhaps best known for his 'ecological systems model', now redefined as the 'bioecological model'.

KEY PUBLICATIONS

Bronfenbrenner, U. (1979) *The Ecology of Human Development*. Cambridge, MA: Harvard University Press.

Bronfenbrenner, U. and Ceci, S.J. (1994) 'Nature–nurture reconceptualized in the developmental perspective: a bioecological model', *Psychological Review*, 101: 568–86.

UNDERSTANDING THE THEORY

THE ECOLOGICAL SYSTEMS MODEL

Unlike theorists before him, Bronfenbrenner widened his focus to include those crucial political, economic and social factors that impact on children's development and learning. This is key to understanding his theory. Bronfenbrenner believed that it was especially helpful to view children's development and learning through the notion of layers, sometimes likened to those of a Russian doll (see diagram below). He suggested that these layers impact directly and indirectly on the biological maturation of every child. His theory, therefore, emphasizes the importance of examining the wider environmental influences on children's learning (Gray and MacBlain, 2015). Bronfenbrenner named each of these layers, with the closest and most immediate to the child being the 'microsystem'.

The microsystem refers to children's most immediate contacts, for example their family, playgroup, neighbours and local communities. Bronfenbrenner suggested a two-way process or 'bi-directional

Microsystem: immediate environments such as the family, nursery school, playgroup, peers and local community

Mesosystem: a system comprising connections between children's immediate environments such as their home and their school

Exosystem: external environmental settings that indirectly affect development, for example the workplace of the child's parents

Macrosystem: the larger cultural context, for example different world cultures in which children grow up, and political and economic contexts

Chronosystem: the patterning of environmental events and transitions over children's lives

Bronfenbrenner's ecological model of individual development

Source: Based on Bronfenbrenner (1979)

influences' within the microsystem that influence children. What he is suggesting by this is that whilst children are influenced by the behaviours and actions of others, they, in turn, also influence the behaviours and actions of those they come into contact with. Consider, for example, how a young child who enjoys entertaining others can actively change their behaviour.

Outside of the microsystem is the 'mesosystem', which is to do with connections between, for example, a child's parents and the adults working in their playgroup or nursery. Children begin to make simple comparisons between their experiences at school and those in their home. They can also draw comparisons between their friends at school and those friends where they live, as well as their siblings.

Next to the mesosystem is the 'exosystem' or wider social systems; the exosystem refers to children's cultures, the values of the society in which they live, wider legal structures, and so on – their parents' work commitments and level of income will impact directly and indirectly on the child's microsystem. One example of this system is the increase in early years provision brought about by recent government legislation whereby parents now have far greater choice. Within the next system, the 'macrosystem', ideologies that have been historically dominant in children's cultures become of greater importance. Bronfenbrenner identified a further layer, the 'chronosystem', which attempts to explain how time interfaces with the environments in which children grow up.

THE IMPORTANCE OF CULTURE

Bronfenbrenner placed considerable emphasis on how children develop and learn in constantly changing and evolving cultures where they interact daily with many types of individuals and often in a variety of different settings (Bronfenbrenner, 1979; Bronfenbrenner and Ceci, 1994). He also emphasized the importance of studying children's development within those cultural contexts within which they live, or what he referred to as 'the ecology of development' (Smith et al., 2003, p. 9). Consider the different cultures that children are born into in the UK and how the traditions in these cultures impact on their thinking and how they learn. Importantly, Bronfenbrenner proposed that practitioners working with children in the early years should view them not as a discrete 'early years' group but as developing individuals who are unique and who

are at the beginning stages of a development process ending in adulthood.

WHAT THE THEORY LOOKS LIKE IN PRACTICE

It is possible to explain many of the behaviours one witnesses in schools and early years settings using Bronfenbrenner's theory. From the moment of birth and even prior to birth, children are affected directly and indirectly by external influences in their family, in their community and in the wider society they are born into. Consider, for example, how a child entering an early years setting for the first time is influenced

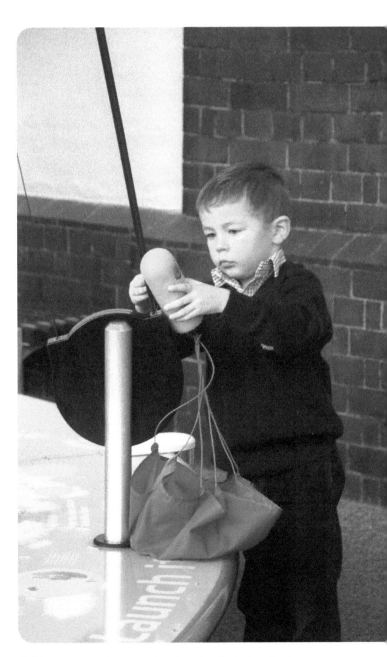

Children need to be understood as developing and unique individuals

by such factors as the physical environment in which the setting is situated – inner city, deprived area, rural countryside, and so on. The same child's experiences of learning and development will also be indirectly impacted on by the level of funding the early years setting receives each year to buy resources and appoint staff. In addition, any new legislation in the field of early years education that is passed by government will have an indirect impact on the child's learning as it may affect the manner in which staff are asked to deliver a curriculum or to work without a curriculum.

CASE STUDY: BI-DIRECTIONAL INFLUENCES

A baby girl is lying in her cot. Suddenly, and for no apparent reason, she makes a loud and very pleasing cooing sound. When her mother hears the sound, she comes running in from the kitchen, picks the baby up, hugs her and gives her lots of attention. Whilst the baby initiated the interaction by making a pleasant sound, the mother has responded. In this way, the baby is influencing and directing her mother's behaviour; Bronfenbrenner would suggest that this pattern of behaviours between the little girl and her mother is bi-directional. He argued that such bi-directional influences are very strong.

CASE STUDY: THE IMMEDIATE ENVIRONMENT – LEARNING AND DEVELOPMENT

Liam is 3 years of age and attends a local playgroup where he is displaying a great deal of aggressive behaviour. The head of the playgroup has referred Liam for an assessment by an educational psychologist. In her referral, she has described Liam as 'constantly seeking attention and overly quick to become tearful. Of late, he has been showing signs of marked aggression towards other children, including a great deal of swearing. He appears to have real difficulties with forming friendships.' Liam lives with his younger brother Matthew, aged 2 years, and his mother who has been out of work for over ten years. Liam's mother has been in a very dysfunctional relationship with Jason for over a year. Jason is frequently aggressive towards Liam's mum and Liam regularly observes Jason striking and punching his mother. Jason is also extremely verbally abusive. Liam gets very upset and frightened when Jason visits their home. Liam has started to imitate Jason's aggressive behaviours, frequently hitting his younger brother. Thomas is also 3 years of age and attends the same playgroup. Thomas is described by the head of the playgroup as 'an extremely able little boy, hardworking and articulate, delightful to be around and good at making friends'. Thomas lives at home with his parents and a younger sister, Zara, aged 2 years. His parents both went to university and have good careers. They have a large circle of friends and interests and work hard to involve their children in activities with friends and family, all of whom are positive role models. If Thomas's parents are cross with him, they will take time to explain their feelings and those behaviours that have caused them to be upset. Thomas has been introduced to simple picture/story books since he was very young. His ability to read words and remain interested in a story is very good and is reflected in his growing enthusiasm for reading. Outside of school, he has many friendship groups. Liam and Thomas have internalized markedly different patterns of behaviour that have been modelled by adults in their families; they each have a very different *microsystem*. Liam's social and emotional learning has been dominated by a lack of positive role modelling. Thomas, on the other hand, has been nurtured within his own *microsystem* and has benefitted from his parents having good jobs, acting intelligently and giving him access to positive experiences. Unlike Thomas, Liam does not have the added security of consistency within his home life where, daily, he experiences aggression, inconsistency and a distinct lack of organization.

STRENGTHS AND WEAKNESSES OF THE THEORY

Bronfenbrenner's theory has a great deal to offer early years practitioners; it is comprehensive in how it offers a focus on wider, more environmental influences on children's development and their learning. Unlike most other theories, it places great emphasis on the degree to which dynamic factors around children impact on their learning and development. Bronfenbrenner's theory has been criticized, however, on the grounds that it does not pay sufficient attention to individual development. That said, it is also possible to assert that his underlying theoretical perspectives complement those theories that have largely failed to place enough focus on the nature of children's learning and development.

LINKS TO OTHER THEORIES

Bronfenbrenner's theory differs from that of Bandura to the extent that he saw factors in the child's wider social, political and economic environment as hugely significant to their learning. Unlike Bandura, he believed that children's own biology is a key influential factor in their development and learning. Like Bandura and Vygotsky, Bronfenbrenner saw the cultures in which children grow up as playing a significant part in their education and learning. Unlike Piaget, he did not place so much emphasis on the idea of children progressing through stages.

> ### ACTIVITIES AND POINTS FOR DISCUSSION
>
> **Activity:** Identify the economic, political and social factors that influence children's education in the UK today. Having done so, arrange these in terms of priority, from those you consider have the greatest impact to the least.
>
> **Discussion Point:** Having created your list and prioritized the degree of impact, discuss why there may have been disagreement with others and why disagreement exists amongst practitioners as to what factors in society impact the most on children's learning.

EXTENDED AND RECOMMENDED READING

MacBlain, S.F. and Gray, C. (2016) 'Pioneers: Bandura and Bronfenbrenner explained', *Early Educator*, 18(1): 38–44. (A thorough account of the ideas underpinning Bronfenbrenner's theory and how these complement and contrast with those of Bandura.)

Pugh, G. and Duffy, B. (2014) *Contemporary Issues in the Early Years* (6th edn). London: Sage. (A comprehensive account of early years policy and practice in the UK.)

REFERENCES

Bronfenbrenner, U. (1979) *The Ecology of Human Development*. Cambridge, MA: Harvard University Press.

Bronfenbrenner, U. and Ceci, S.J. (1994) 'Nature–nurture reconceptualized in the developmental perspective: a bioecological model', *Psychological Review*, 101: 568–86.

Gray, C. and MacBlain, S.F. (2015) *Learning Theories in Childhood* (2nd edn). London: Sage.

Smith, K.S., Cowie, H. and Blades, M. (2003) *Understanding Children's Development* (4th edn). Oxford: Blackwell.

JEROME BRUNER AND CONSTRUCTIVISM

THE THEORIST (1915–2016)

Jerome Bruner was born in 1915 in New York, USA and is considered to be one of the leading contributors to our understanding of learning. Though initially a psychologist, Bruner became an established figure in the field of education and developed new ways of thinking about children's learning. Bruner's purpose in developing his theoretical perspective was largely driven by his need to challenge the thinking of his time, which was dominated by the traditions of psychodynamics and behaviourism, originating in the works of Sigmund Freud, and Pavlov and Skinner.

KEY PUBLICATIONS

Bruner, J. (1960) *The Process of Education*. Cambridge, MA: Harvard University Press.

Bruner, J. (1996) *Culture of Education*. Cambridge, MA: Harvard University Press.

UNDERSTANDING THE THEORY

Central to Bruner's theory of learning is the notion of *instrumental conceptualism*, which has three key elements: acquiring new information or knowledge; transforming and manipulating knowledge; and checking knowledge. Bruner based his theory of learning on two fundamental assertions, the first being that children's knowledge of the world is based on models of reality that they construct, and the second that these models are initially adopted from their own cultures, which they then adapt for their own future use.

Bruner rejected many of the theories of learning that influenced practice in school at the time, preferring instead to emphasize how children might and should become more involved in their own learning. His ideas on learning and how these contrasted with other theories of learning were encapsulated some decades ago by Brown

Acquiring new knowledge begins at even the earliest stages of development

(1977, p.74) who suggested that Bruner viewed research into children's learning in problem-solving situations as being overly focused on the type of tasks and stimuli presented to them, with not enough emphasis being given to the 'dynamic qualities' that each child brought to such tasks when attempting to solve them

HOW CHILDREN THINK

Bruner argued that children represent their worlds through three modes, which he called the *enactive*, *iconic* and *symbolic* modes. The first refers to actions, the second to images and pictures, and the third to words and symbols. The three modes do not follow in succession, as was the case with Piaget's idea of successive stages. Instead, they are integrated with one another and their use is linked to the level of experience the child has.

Bruner was particularly concerned with how stimuli are represented by children as symbols and words, how these representations change with experience, and how they connect with existing concepts which lead to generalization. The representation of stimuli through symbols such as words was, for Bruner, of a much higher order than images. He saw the inferences that children make through words and symbols as being key to their learning.

THE ENACTIVE MODE

With the *enactive* mode, an infant's view of an object becomes linked with their physical movements. Consider a very young baby lying in a cot who is offered a rattle by her mother. The baby shakes the rattle, which makes a noise, and in so doing the baby is alerted to the noise. Whenever the child is again offered the rattle, she will shake it; over time, her physical movements will come to be linked to the noise and to the actual rattle, and will become gradually encoded within her memory store through what psychologists and teachers commonly refer to as 'kinaesthetic memory'.

THE ICONIC MODE

With the *iconic* mode, Bruner proposed that children internally represent objects within their thinking as images and in so doing progress their thinking significantly. Being able to store images means that children can extend their thinking to objects which are not immediately present in their environment. Bruner acknowledged that this mode has limitations, as images

held by the child are, for example, restricted to specific observable features such as colour, smell and texture. Though children can represent images of objects and images of people around them internally such as their parents and siblings, the *iconic* mode falls short of allowing them to internally represent more abstract concepts such as kindness and happiness. To do this, they require language, which will then allow them to represent such concepts within their thinking; it is this important element that is central to the *symbolic* mode.

THE SYMBOLIC MODE

The difference between the *iconic* mode and symbols that are central to the *symbolic* mode can be understood as follows: A picture of a cow is an icon as it represents the animal in a real manner; the symbols 'C', 'O', 'W', however, demonstrate the existence of this animal because the combination of these letters has been accepted by everyone (Brown, 1977)

As children's abilities with language develop, they can physically remove themselves from situations and still think about them. They can also engage verbally with others and talk in increasingly sophisticated ways

The joys of written language can begin at even the earliest of stages

about situations that are not immediately present to them or about events they believe might occur in the future. Importantly, they can engage with others in problem solving and reflection, which Bruner argued are two of the most crucial features, central to the development of thinking and, more specifically, higher order thinking skills.

THE IMPORTANCE OF STRATEGIES

Bruner was particularly interested in the types of strategies used by children when they engage in learning new tasks, and especially when learning involves problem-solving activities. He suggested that the thinking (internal cognitive structures) of children who engage a lot with reading and writing will typically differ from those children who mostly absorb themselves with activities that are much less language-oriented, such as drawing and construction (Brown, 1977).

THE IMPORTANCE OF LANGUAGE

Bruner suggested that children who engage a great deal with adults and older peers through spoken language typically differ from those children who do not. His reasoning for this was that young children naturally engage in verbal interaction with those around them anyway. This type of 'natural' engagement may not, like that of verbal interaction with adults, extend and progress their abilities to internally represent thinking through vocabulary and more complicated language structures. He also suggested that when

Through spoken and written language, children learn to represent concepts in their thinking

Reading and writing offer opportunities for deeper reflection children actively engage in writing with purpose, a fundamental transformative process occurs, whereby the children can then engage in deeper reflection and critical analysis of their own ideas and those of others.

SCAFFOLDING

The term *scaffolding*, though developed by Bruner, was originally coined by Wood et al. (1976, cited in Gray and MacBlain, 2015, p. 6). This process, whereby adults work alongside children to support and progress their learning, can be extremely effective and highly motivating for children. Amongst the many benefits of scaffolding is the important fact that, rather than being a rigid process, it is very flexible and can be employed by practitioners in almost any setting with very positive results.

DISCOVERY LEARNING

Bruner placed great emphasis on *discovery learning*, where adults create environments with the aim of offering children meaningful and purposeful opportunities to apply their own resources and learn through exploration. In this way, they can extend the cognitive capacity and functioning of the children, both of which lie at the very heart of learning. Much of course depends on the situations that are created, and it almost goes without saying that different situations and activities yield different results.

WHAT THE THEORY LOOKS LIKE IN PRACTICE

It is possible to observe, on a daily basis, the ideas that are central to Bruner's theory being put into practice in early years settings, at primary school and in the home. Often, this is done without adults being fully aware that the activities children are engaged in reflect the underlying principles of Bruner's theory. For example, Bruner argued strongly that the level of interest children have in a subject is one of the key factors in their learning and that motivating children is a key function of the work of teachers and practitioners.

Every day, practitioners in early years settings create activities that excite children and encourage them to work collaboratively to construct new ideas and new thinking. Indeed, the excitement of young children being introduced to a new topic can often be described as almost tangible.

New environments lead to new discoveries and new learning

Bruner also emphasized the importance of teachers knowing what existing knowledge children have and then building on this – the notion of a 'spiral' curriculum where adults provide children with choice and create opportunities for them to develop their vocabulary, the types of sentences they use and how they listen to others and contribute to group activities, for example with creative play. Now consider the following two case studies, which demonstrate key elements of Bruner's theory in practice.

CASE STUDY: CONSTRUCTIVISM IN ACTION

It is a cold and frosty day and Ms Malik takes her group of pre-school children outside to explore the ice and frost that have formed during the night. Along with the other adults, she encourages the children to make marks in the frost and look closely at the patterns that have formed in the frozen puddles on the ground. The children are encouraged to use new words spoken by the adults, such as 'sparkling' and 'slippery', as they experience the physical impact on their senses of the cold and the slipperiness underfoot.

When they return inside, the children are encouraged to take pieces of ice with them and then drop different coloured dyes on to the ice and observe the patterns that form. Again, new words are offered by the adults to increase the children's vocabulary and to give them the language tools to extend their thinking. The children are then encouraged to use these new words and to ask new questions of the adults to support them in understanding the physical nature of the ice and the process by which water comes to be frozen. They are also encouraged to engage in problem solving and investigating 'ice' further, using relevant books and pictures.

CASE STUDY: THE SYMBOLIC MODE IN PRACTICE

The teacher gives a group of children one piece of A4 paper and a book and challenges them to stand the piece of paper on its side and balance the book on top. She is interested in how they cooperate to complete the task, the strategies they employ and their use of language. She listens as they begin:

Cara: This is stupid, it's silly. We can't do this.
Fiona: Wait, I think we could change the shape of the paper.
Nicola: Yes, good idea. What if we fold the paper like in a zigzag shape?
Fiona: Yes. Turn the paper on its side in a zigzag and then we can balance the book on top. That makes the paper stronger.

This example is a good illustration of children constructing meaning at the symbolic level. By starting her sentence with, 'Wait, I think we could…' Fiona has begun to engage in logical reasoning, which is of a much higher order than Cara's response, which is only a reaction to the problem. Fiona's hypothesis is tested not just by her attempts at physically manipulating the paper but also, importantly, by the responses of her peers. For example, Nicola has agreed to Fiona's suggestion to alter the shape of the paper, thereby confirming her logical thinking and hypothesis. By further suggesting that they could make a concertina shape with the paper, she has extended and progressed Fiona's thinking and built on Fiona's existing knowledge.

STRENGTHS AND WEAKNESSES OF THE THEORY

Bruner's theory has much to offer practitioners in the early years. It places children at the heart of the learning experience, emphasizes the importance of language and social interaction, and the progression of thinking through constructing new understanding. Criticisms have been levelled at Bruner's ideas, however, particularly his notion of discovery learning. It has been argued, for example, that when given opportunities to engage in learning through discovery, children may acquire misconceptions which go unnoticed by their teachers and which then distort aspects of their future learning. A further criticism is that, whilst discovery learning suits the learning styles of some children, it may not be the most appropriate for other children, who may, for example, prefer a more didactic way of learning. There are also those parents and schools who would perceive this way of learning as a poor use of children's time, preferring instead to use the time in a more formal way with the children being 'taught directly' by teachers.

LINKS TO OTHER THEORIES

Like Piaget, Bruner believed that learning should be a process of social interaction in which children are active participants and involve themselves fully, for example in problem solving. Unlike Piaget, however, who placed far greater emphasis on the environment, Bruner saw the role of the teacher as being central to children's learning. In contrast to the behaviourists, Bruner was more concerned with what happens 'inside' children's minds between a stimulus being emitted and children making their responses. Behaviourists, he felt, had really concerned themselves too much with how children react to stimuli. Like Vygotsky, he viewed children's learning as a social activity, which could be progressed through language and instruction from others, for example parents and teachers. Bruner developed Vygotsky's idea of learning as a social activity, suggesting, for example, that children can be observed everywhere learning alongside adults who structure activities for them within varying social contexts.

ACTIVITIES AND POINTS FOR DISCUSSION

Activity: Give one piece of A4 paper and a book to a group of children and challenge them to balance the book on the edge of the paper. Observe their attempts and try to identify the vocabulary and sentences they use to communicate their ideas to one another (the symbolic mode). (If they are successful, they will fold the sheet of paper in a concertina shape and turn it on its side, which will enable them to balance the book.)

Discussion Points: Identify examples of 'scaffolding' that you might have observed and then consider the following:

1. Could children have learned just as well without an adult being involved?
2. How can language be used to support scaffolding in young children?

EXTENDED AND RECOMMENDED READING

Bruce, T. (2011) *Early Childhood Education* (4th edn). London: Hodder. (A comprehensive and accessible account of early childhood.)

Gray, C. and MacBlain, S.F. (2015) *Learning Theories in Childhood* (2nd edn). London: Sage. (Chapter 8 is a very readable and informative chapter on the ideas of Bruner and how these relate to practice in the early years.)

MacBlain, S.F. and Bowman, H. (2016) 'Teaching and learning', in D. Wyse and S. Rogers (eds), *A Guide to Early Years and Primary Teaching*. London: Sage. (An informative chapter that focuses on what makes for good practice in children's learning at primary school and in early years settings.)

REFERENCES

Brown, G. (1977) *Child Development*. Shepton Mallet: Open Books.

Gray, C. and MacBlain, S.F. (2015) *Learning Theories in Childhood* (2nd edn). London: Sage.

Wood, D., Bruner, J.S. and Ross, G. (1976) 'The role of tutoring in problem solving', *Journal of Child Psychology and Psychiatry*, 17(2): 81–100.

HOWARD GARDNER AND THEORIES OF MULTIPLE INTELLIGENCE

THE THEORIST (1943 – PRESENT)

Howard Gardner's ideas on the nature of intelligence have had a significant impact on how many now view children's thinking and learning. Gardner studied under the notable theorist Jerome Bruner and for a while worked with him. Bruner also had an enormous influence on Gardner and particularly the way in which he sought to explain learning and intellectual development in children. Gardner was also influenced by the renowned psychoanalyst Erik Erikson, under whom he also studied when a student at Harvard University.

KEY PUBLICATIONS

Gardner, H. (1975) *The Shattered Mind.* New York: Knopf.

Gardner, H. (2006) *Changing Minds: The Art and Science of Changing Our Own and Other People's Minds.* Boston, MA: Harvard Business School Press.

UNDERSTANDING THE THEORY

To fully comprehend Gardner's theory of 'multiple intelligences', it is useful first to understand some of the background to how intelligence has been understood and explained in the past. One of the most controversial areas in the psychology of human development is that of 'intelligence'. For centuries, theorists and philosophers have argued about what intelligence is and, perhaps most controversially, whether it is inherited and can be measured.

WHAT IS INTELLIGENCE?

Two decades ago, Nicky Hayes (1994, cited in MacBlain, 2014, p. 136) emphasized how there are very different opinions as to what intelligence is and how it develops. She proposed that a key factor for such difference was to do with the political implications that intelligence theory has and, in particular, three issues: social stratification, education and eugenics. Hayes surmised that societies in the industrialized West had increasingly adopted a meritocratic system whereby much greater value was given to education and, through

We can observe examples of children applying their intelligence almost everywhere

this process, greater value was then attached to the notion of 'intelligence' and whether or not it was inherited. The extreme nature of some of the opinions about the nature of intelligence in previous generations was offered by Hayes (1994, p. 180) who made reference to the ideas proposed by the Victorian psychologist and eugenicist Francis Galton who believed that the intelligence of the nation would be reduced because the 'lower classes' were producing too many children who would turn out to be generally unintelligent and 'degenerates'.

Since Galton's time, theorists working in the field of psychology have offered more sensible explanations as to what is the nature of intelligence. Some years ago, Gross (1992, p. 840) offered some useful definitions provided by key figures who sought to define intelligence:

- Binet (1905): 'It seems to us that in intelligence there is a fundamental faculty … This faculty is called judgement, otherwise called good sense, practical sense, initiative, the faculty of adapting one's self to circumstances.'

- Terman (1921): 'An individual is intelligent in proportion as he is able to carry on abstract thinking.'

- Burt (1955): 'Innate, general, cognitive ability.'

- Wechsler (1944): 'The aggregate of the global capacity to act purposefully, think rationally, to deal effectively with the environment.'

In more recent years, the notion of intelligence as one unitary concept, which can be measured in the form of an intelligence quotient (IQ), has lost credibility amongst many academics, researchers and practitioners, and has been challenged on the grounds that it is an unreliable construct that fails to account fully for the complexities of individual functioning and such aspects as creativity, motivation, confidence, and so on. In challenging contemporary notions of what intelligence is, Gardner (1983) offered an attractive alternative to viewing intelligence as a unitary entity. In so doing, he also challenged the idea of individuals having an intelligence quotient or IQ. Gardner suggested that intelligence is in fact made up of multiple intelligences and whilst each of these can be understood as systems in their own right, they also interact with each other.

MULTIPLE INTELLIGENCES

Gardner's multiple intelligences can be summarized as follows:

- **Linguistic**: Children employ language to analyse information and, for example, to produce their own books, poems and stories, to relate stories to their peers or adults and to offer explanations when asked questions.

- **Logical-mathematical**: Children demonstrate their ability to work on numerical operations such as calculations, equations and abstract mathematical problems.

- **Spatial**: Children demonstrate their ability to recognize and operate spatial images – for example, in the early stages of writing such as mark making and drawing, or putting jigsaws together.

- **Musical**: Children demonstrate their ability to produce and recall patterns of sound and subsequently make meaning of the sounds and patterns they are creating.

- **Bodily-kinaesthetic**: Children demonstrate their ability to express themselves physically in the use of their bodies and, for example, when making and creating things and even when solving problems. Readers may reflect here on how much human interaction and communication take place non-verbally and through our bodies.

- **Interpersonal**: Children demonstrate their ability to recognize, comprehend and interpret the feelings of others around them, which would include others' intentions, moods and wishes.

- **Intrapersonal**: Children demonstrate their ability to recognize, comprehend and interpret their own feelings and moods as they arise and as they interact with the world around them and with others.

- **Naturalist**: Children demonstrate their ability to recognize and distinguish groups, for example plants and animals and the different environments in their natural world.

Gardner's theory proposes that children who show strengths in one area of intelligence may not necessarily show similar levels of strength in other areas of intelligence. Some theorists have argued that intelligence is highly influenced by environmental factors, whilst others hold that we

CASE STUDY: REALISING THE POTENTIAL WE ARE BORN WITH

Jamie has been born with a very high level of bodily-kinaesthetic intelligence, which has enabled him to quickly develop intricate movements combining hand and foot actions. This means that when he was introduced to activities at his playgroup that involved dancing steps, he was quickly able to master these with little apparent effort. His peers, on the other hand, required much practice. He is quickly singled out by the adults in his playgroup as being very able. Though his peers will eventually master the dance steps and become very proficient with these, Jamie is able to employ his natural bodily-kinaesthetic intelligence as opposed to having to spend much time and effort on practising. His abilities in developing written skills and numerical operations are, on the other hand, quite limited and, unlike many of his peers, he struggles with this aspect of learning.

CASE STUDY: REALIZING OUR INTELLIGENCE

Noah and Jack have both been born with a natural ability in music. From an early age, they both appear to be very interested in music and are observed to enjoy sitting and listening intently to adults who play musical instruments. When given instruments to play themselves, they quickly become absorbed and both can keep tempos and follow rhythms. In the years that follow, Jack's parents encourage him to develop his musical talents; they buy him a small guitar and arrange for him to have lessons with a tutor. Noah, on the other hand, receives little encouragement from his parents and gradually loses interest in developing his skills. In the years that follow, Jack takes up music as a subject specialism at secondary school and develops his skills and knowledge base in music so that he can perform in front of others to a very high standard. Noah does not.

inherit innate intelligence and can do little to change it. Gardner, by contrast, argued that intelligence is an amalgamation of abilities, potential and skills that are inherited and that can, importantly, be extended through pertinent and significant experiences.

1. '8 Intelligences: Theory of Multiple Intelligences Explained – Dr. Howard Gardner': www.youtube. com/watch?v=s2EdujrM0vA
2. 'Multiple Intelligences Thrive in Smartville': www. youtube.com/watch?v=7zBKAT3le_s

WHAT THE THEORY LOOKS LIKE IN PRACTICE

It is possible to observe Gardner's theory of multiple intelligences in practice in most early years settings, where practitioners take as given the fact that children progress and learn in different ways and with appropriate support can develop their potential and the dispositions they have been born with. Practitioners will also be familiar with children who present with natural abilities in music or art but experience significant challenges with other aspects of learning, for example literacy or numeracy. Take time to view the following two YouTube videos, which offer many examples of Gardner's theory of multiple intelligences in practice:

STRENGTHS AND WEAKNESSES OF THE THEORY

Gardner's ideas on the nature of intelligence have had a significant impact on how we view children's thinking and learning. In many respects, he has offered the field of education an exciting and quite different way of viewing children's intellectual development. His ideas have been embraced by many teachers and early years practitioners, who have often viewed them as a refreshing means of identifying potential in those children with whom they work. Gardner's theory has, however, been criticized on the grounds that it is not possible to quantify and test elements of his theory. For example, it is argued that it is not possible to be clear as to how the different intelligences can operate separately or how they might, in practice, interact with each other (MacBlain, 2014).

LINKS TO OTHER THEORIES

Gardner's theory has some similarities with the ideas put forward by Reuven Feuerstein. Both viewed intelligence as something that can be changed and both have taken a very positive view of the possibilities that language can provide for developing those innate dispositions that children are born with. Gardner's ideas also find support amongst followers of Bruner and Vygotsky, both of whom saw the valuable role that adults can play in supporting and extending children's abilities and potential.

ACTIVITIES AND POINTS FOR DISCUSSION

Activity: List a range of activities that you have observed children to be involved in and decide how they might demonstrate each of Gardner's *intelligences*.

Discussion Point: Why might those adults who are less familiar with learning in young children continue to view intelligence as something we are all born with and that can be measured by using tests?

EXTENDED AND RECOMMENDED READING

Gardner, H., Csikszentmihalyi, M. and Damon, W. (2001) *Good Work: Where Excellence and Ethics Meet.* New York: Basic Books. (A comprehensive text.)

MacBlain, S.F. (2014) *How Children Learn.* London: Sage. (See, in particular, Chapter 6 on intelligence.)

REFERENCES

Gardner, H. (1983) *Frames of Mind.* London: Fontana. Gross, R.D. (1992) *Psychology: The Science of Mind and Behaviour* (2nd edn). London: Hodder & Stoughton.

Hayes, N. (1994) *Foundations of Psychology: An Introductory Text.* London: Routledge.

MacBlain, S.F. (2014) *How Children Learn.* London: Sage.

REUVEN FEUERSTEIN AND INSTRUMENTAL ENRICHMENT

THE THEORIST (1921–2014)

Reuven Feuerstein was born in Botosani, Romania in 1921, and following the end of World War II worked with child survivors of the Holocaust. This experience shaped his thinking in regard to how children think and learn. When these child survivors were initially assessed by Feuerstein using standardized intelligence (IQ) tests, he observed that they did not perform well, though when he began working with them on an individual basis he found they did much better than their test scores suggested, and more particularly that their performance improved significantly. This led him to investigate how these children learned and to question whether their intellectual abilities were, in fact, 'fixed' from birth. He then began exploring the difference between assessing children's abilities through individual standardized tests and assessing their potential.

KEY PUBLICATION

Feuerstein, R., Rand, Y., Hoffman, M. and Miller, R. (1980) *Instrumental Enrichment*. Baltimore, MD: University Park Press.

UNDERSTANDING THE THEORY

Feuerstein proposed that the belief systems we have about children's learning and their intellectual development ought to view human potential as having almost no limits. He suggested that artificial barriers are often in place that prevent change in how children learn and, more particularly, how they might realize their potential. Feuerstein argued that all children, no matter what their degree of difficulty, can, with appropriate support, become effective learners. In adopting such belief systems, practitioners can then, he believed, be freed from the sort of restricted thinking that limits their vision of what might be possible for them to achieve with every child. When

this type of approach is adopted by practitioners working with children, certain consequences take place in children's thinking, a process Feuerstein called 'structural cognitive modifiability'. This refers to the notion that the cognitive structure of a child's brain can be altered through an enabling process that supports children in learning how to learn. Learning, therefore, becomes cumulative and impacts positively on children's learning for the rest of their lives (Burden, 1987). Such an approach, in effect, alters the structural nature of children's cognitive development.

Feuerstein argued that the central feature involved in learning how to learn is the process of the 'mediated learning experience'. Feuerstein et al. (1980, p. 16) referred to this process as:

> the way in which stimuli emitted by the environment are transferred by a 'mediating' agent, usually a parent, sibling or other caregiver. This mediated agent, guided by his intentions, culture, and emotional investment, selects and organises the world of stimuli for the child … Through this process of mediation, the cognitive structure of the child is affected.

A child's potential for learning has almost no limits

A core feature of this way of learning is how the teacher or mediator ensures that children understand what is expected of them; mediators should, therefore, take great care, for example, when explaining to children why they are being asked to work on particular activities. They should also ensure that children understand that the activities they are being asked to engage in have actual value beyond what they are being asked to do.

WHAT THE THEORY LOOKS LIKE IN PRACTICE

View the YouTube video, 'Feuerstein Institute – Step Forward': www.youtube.com/watch?v=Th9nw99Kw-4&list=PLyHTdVRj_jrpMSgOGXnXF42T2-bDHXZqH&index=2, which offers many examples of Feuerstein's theory in practice.

STRENGTHS AND WEAKNESSES OF THE THEORY

A major strength of Feuerstein's theory is that it places children's potential for learning at the very heart of their interactions with adults. In emphasizing the distinction between 'ability' and 'potential', Feuerstein recognized the importance of adults creating learning environments where children could come to realize their potential, as opposed to simply working to perceived abilities. Feuerstein also drew an important distinction between 'static' assessment and 'dynamic assessment'; the former refers to such assessments as those found in test situations familiar to many readers, when a child is tested on a particular day at a particular time with test results being accepted as an 'accurate' measure of their capabilities. With dynamic assessment, on the other hand, assessment takes place over time, with a much greater emphasis being given to children's potential to learn with guidance and support. Consider the case where a child's reading is tested on a particular day and a reading age score recorded and decisions then made as a result of the child's actual reading score, as opposed to the child's potential to read more effectively if given a different approach to reading and the support of an adult. With dynamic assessment, the child could be asked to attempt a literacy task, and after their result is recorded they are then given a number of strategies by their teacher to help develop the particular thinking skills that are required when decoding new words, as with practice in blending sounds.

LINKS TO OTHER THEORIES

Feuerstein's theory has many similarities with those of Vygotsky and Bruner in that they all placed considerable emphasis on the construction of knowledge and view the role of the teacher as being one of promoting the development of children's thinking through providing support. Like Vygotsky and Bruner, Feuerstein placed great emphasis on the importance of language and how it facilitates and develops thinking skills.

ACTIVITIES AND POINTS FOR DISCUSSION

Activity: View the YouTube video, 'Down Syndrome Film "Looking Up On Down" (Glow Films/Feuerstein Institute film by David Goodwin)': www.youtube.com/watch?v=lqSQI6VJgLk, and identify the key aspects of Feuerstein's ideas that are seen by the family in the video clip as being helpful for their child's learning.

Discussion Point: Consider how early years practitioners can mediate with children with special educational needs and/or disabilities to develop the children's thinking skills and, in so doing, support them in developing their potential.

EXTENDED AND RECOMMENDED READING

Burden, R.L. (1987) 'Feuerstein's instrumental enrichment programme: important issues in research and evaluation', *European Journal of Psychology of Education*, 2(1): 3–16.

MacBlain, S.F. (2014) *How Children Learn*. London: Sage. (Chapter 6.)

REFERENCES

Burden, R.L. (1987) 'Feuerstein's instrumental enrichment programme: important issues in research and evaluation', *European Journal of Psychology of Education*, 2(1): 3–16.

Feuerstein, R., Rand, Y., Hoffman, M. and Miller, R. (1980) *Instrumental Enrichment*. Baltimore, MD: University Park Press.

NEL NODDINGS AND THE ETHICS OF CARE

THE THEORIST (1929 – PRESENT)

Nel Noddings was born in New Jersey, USA. She is an educationalist and philosopher and is perhaps best known for her ideas on the philosophy of education, in particular educational theory and the ethics of care. She spent a number of years working in schools in the USA as a teacher and administrator before entering academia.

KEY PUBLICATIONS

Noddings, N. (1984) *Caring: A Feminine Approach to Ethics and Moral Education*. Berkeley, CA: University of California Press.

Noddings, N. (1996) 'Stories and affect in teacher education', *Cambridge Journal of Education*, 26(3): 435–47.

UNDERSTANDING THE THEORY

Noddings (1984, 1996, 1999, 2005a, 2005b) introduced us to what is a most appealing way of thinking about children's learning in the early years, focusing on the issue of ethics and how this relates to

Care in the first years is essential to future learning

'care'. She has particularly addressed the importance of relationships and how care relates to education, how children learn within their families and communities, and learning in early years settings and primary schools. Noddings emphasized how the home is at the core of children's education and has voiced her desire for greater recognition being given to the important role that the home plays in children's early development and learning.

RELATIONAL CARING

Noddings drew a distinction between two types of caring relevant to teachers and practitioners in the early years, emphasizing that all teachers who work with children 'care' in some sense, though not in another. Some teachers, she argues, care in the 'virtue' sense – in other words, they are conscientious in what they do, follow goals and objectives for their children and work hard at inspiring children to achieve these goals and do well academically. However, she also suggests that some teachers 'may be unable to establish relations of care and trust' in a 'relational sense', where they bring to their work with children high levels of empathy and view each child as a wholly unique individual.

Noddings proposed that some teachers and practitioners in education might find difficulty in accepting her notion of relational caring due, in part, to a strong legacy in education of teachers feeling they know best. She emphasized, however, that it is also now unacceptable for teachers and practitioners to assume that they know best. Importantly, Noddings also placed emphasis on the nature of the challenges facing many teachers and early years practitioners today, suggesting that the complex nature of some children's conditions can work against the formation of caring relations (MacBlain, 2014). She proposed that this could, in part, be due to such factors as pressures associated with large class sizes, the nature of the curricula many children are expected to follow, and the external requirements of teachers and practitioners that they test children and achieve targets.

CASE STUDY: BUILDING TRUST

Natalie has started working in a Key Stage 1 class and has been made aware that some of the children in her class have experienced significant social and emotional difficulties emanating from their home backgrounds. She has spent time studying the work of Nel Noddings and is aware of two key factors deriving from the work of Noddings that she needs to introduce into her teaching to help her support these children. First, Natalie is aware that she needs to actively listen to, not just hear, her children when they speak about themselves. In this way, she feels she must aim to try to gain their trust, which will form the basis of the relationship she will have with them as their teacher. She will aim to be cooperative with the children when they are engaging in learning tasks and to hold back from interfering when they are engaged in learning or in collaboration tasks with their peers that promote learning.

CASE STUDY: BUILDING PRACTICE THROUGH LISTENING TO CHILDREN'S NEEDS

Natalie further decides to develop her teaching along the lines she has read when studying the work of Nel Noddings. Whenever possible, she will engage the children in dialogue as a means of learning about their own individual needs, how they work and the strengths they have in learning as well as their weaknesses. This, she believes, will help her to build her teaching in such a way that the children will increasingly see real value in what she is doing with them.

WHAT THE THEORY LOOKS LIKE IN PRACTICE

Teachers and practitioners working with children in the early years today actively endeavour to develop their skills in listening to children. They are open to empathizing with their children and in a way that the children will come to trust them with their feelings and emotions. Practitioners also seek to set aside time when they are free from distractions and can listen attentively to any concerns being expressed by the children, without being interrupted. Practitioners work to promote within themselves attitudes to their work with the children that are underpinned by empathy and a desire to know their children as fully as possible and to understand their unique and individual holistic needs.

STRENGTHS AND WEAKNESSES OF THE THEORY

Noddings believed that the chief aim of education is to create caring, confident, loving and lovable individuals. She placed considerable emphasis on the importance of the home, which for most, if not all, practitioners in the early years is seen as central to their work with children. She offered practitioners a refreshing and relevant means of understanding the importance of care in the lives of young children. Practitioners working particularly with children from dysfunctional families will, all too readily, understand the absolute importance of care in the lives of young children and the detrimental impact that a lack of care can have.

Noddings' emphasis on the 'ethics of care' has been criticized by some feminists who suggest that her approach is overly masculine, in that it suggests that the caring of young children is viewed as a traditional female role which is predominantly about giving, whilst receiving little back; this view suggests an unequal view of relationships and, therefore, a model of care that is unhelpful. A further critical interpretation of Noddings' ideas on the ethics of care in young children is that the carer is the dominant person in the relationship with the cared-for being largely dependent and, therefore, having little if any control over the type of caring they receive (Hoagland, 1990).

LINKS TO OTHER THEORIES

Noddings' ideas have many similarities to those of theorists who sought to place children's social and emotional development at the heart of learning. In this respect, she can be likened to Rousseau, Pestalozzi and Froebel, amongst others. Like these early theorists and those who promoted the ideas of Freud, she placed enormous emphasis on the importance of the family and the need for children to have love and security in their lives. Like Montessori, Dewey and Bandura, she broached the important area of ethical considerations in the lives of young children, with attention being given to the role of the teacher and, like Steiner practitioners, the quality of those relationships that teachers and others create and maintain with their children.

ACTIVITIES AND POINTS FOR DISCUSSION

Activity: Take time to view the YouTube video, 'Nel Noddings Theorist Film' by Krista Roe: www.youtube.com/watch?v=RrBpZFdeoVE. Then, make a list of those factors you consider contribute to good levels of 'care' in young children, prioritizing those that you believe to be the most important.

Discussion Point: Having identified factors that contribute to good levels of care in young children, discuss what factors in society might prevent these being present in children's lives and what early years practitioners can do to support children who fail to have good levels of care in their lives.

EXTENDED AND RECOMMENDED READING

James, A. and Prout, A. (2015) *Constructing and Reconstructing Childhood: Contemporary Issues in the Sociological Study of Childhood*. London: Routledge. (A comprehensive and accessible exploration of childhood today, which explores a range of relevant issues.)

Noddings, N. (2005) 'Caring in education', *The Encyclopaedia of Informal Education*. Available at: http://infed.org/mobi/caring-in-education (06.11.2017).

Sorin, R. (2005) 'Changing images of childhood: reconceptualising early childhood practice', *International Journal of Transitions in Childhood*, 1: 12–21. (An interesting look at the changing nature of childhood.)

REFERENCES

Hoagland, S.L. (1990) 'Some concerns about Nel Noddings' "Caring"', *Hypatia*, 5(1): 109–14.

MacBlain, S.F. (2014) *How Children Learn*. London: Sage.

Noddings, N. (1984) *Caring: A Feminine Approach to Ethics and Moral Education*. Berkeley, CA: University of California Press.

Noddings, N. (1996) 'Stories and affect in teacher education', *Cambridge Journal of Education*, 26(3): 435–47.

Noddings, N. (1999) *Justice and Caring: The Search for Common Ground in Education*. New York: Teachers College Press.

Noddings, N. (2005a) 'Identifying and responding to needs in teacher education', *Cambridge Journal of Education*, 35(2): 147–59.

Noddings, N. (2005b) 'What does it mean to educate the whole child?', *Educational Leadership*, 63(1): 8–13.

TE WHĀRIKI

THE THEORY (1996 – PRESENT)

This approach to young children's learning was originally devised in New Zealand in 1996 with a subsequent revision by the New Zealand government in 2017; its philosophy lies at the heart of the curriculum advocated by the New Zealand government for children in their early years and is at the centre of current practice in early years education in that country.

KEY PUBLICATION

Kanako Murata, K. (2014) *New Zealand Overview and Recent Issues of New Zealand Early Childhood Education Curriculum (Te Whāriki)*. Child Research Net. Available at: www.childresearch.net/projects/ecec/2014_04.html (05.11.2017).

UNDERSTANDING THE THEORY

The Te Whāriki approach is not prescriptive but instead takes into account the experiences and learning that children have in their homes and in

their communities. It emphasizes the importance of children having a strong sense of belonging within their families and communities, as well as happiness and well-being, and puts play and communication at the centre of learning and early development. Due to some words having different meanings and levels of emphasis in the languages of Māori and English, the texts that outline this approach contain words in both languages. The approach is underpinned by four key principles: *Empowerment* (in Māori – *Whakamana*), *Holistic Development* (in Māori – *Kotahitanga*) *Family and Community* (in Māori – *Whānau Tangata*) and *Relationships* (in Māori – *Ngā Hononga*). With the first of these, early years settings aim to provide experiences whereby children from their first years are empowered to learn and develop socially and emotionally. With the second, learning aims to address social and emotional factors, which are viewed as central to holistic development in children. With the third, family and community are recognized as having a strong value in children's learning and development; and with the fourth, positive relationships with others and with places and things are viewed as central to children's learning and development.

Having a sense of belonging is a core feature of effective learning in the early years

WHAT THE THEORY LOOKS LIKE IN PRACTICE

The following five goals lie at the heart of the Te Whāriki approach:

1. The nurturing of children's health, including their emotional health and well-being in situations where they can feel safe and secure (in Māori – *Mana Atua*).

2. Children and their families having a strong sense of belonging (in Māori – *Mana Whenua*), where families and children have links with the wider society in which they live and the wider world valued and affirmed, and where they feel secure with the structures of these communities including the boundaries set along with customs and limits.

3. Contribution (in Māori – *Mana Tangata*), where children are seen as individuals and as equals, and their contributions are valued, irrespective of background.

CASE STUDY: VALUING WELL-BEING

Debbie has begun working in a local playgroup in a district that is characterized by low family incomes, poverty and social deprivation. She notes that a key aim of this setting is to engage children in activities whereby they develop a strong sense of belonging, not only to the setting they are in but also to their local community. Frequent visits take place outside of the playgroup to local areas where the children are encouraged to develop a sense of ownership of their community. On each visit, they are encouraged to meet new people who live within the community and to understand that their community has a great deal to offer.

CASE STUDY: RECOGNITION OF INDIVIDUAL POTENTIAL

In her first weeks working at the playgroup, Debbie becomes quickly aware of the importance that staff place on children realizing their individual potential as opposed to simply developing their literacy and numeracy. Staff at the playgroup take great care to offer each child opportunities whereby they can demonstrate skills that they feel they are good at. In this way, staff are developing the children's self-efficacy, a point greatly emphasized by Albert Bandura (see section on Bandura and Social Learning Theory).

4. Communication (in Māori – *Mana Reo*), where practitioners encourage and facilitate children's own languages in addition to their cultures and the language, symbols, stories and narratives of those cultures. Non-verbal communication is also developed, as are creativity and expression.

5. Exploration (in Māori – *Mana Aotūroa*), where children are encouraged to learn through exploring their environments. Here play is valued as a crucial means of developing confidence and spontaneity in learning. Children learn to exercise control over their bodies and actions and internalize strategies for approaching problem-solving activities that require thinking and, increasingly, logical reasoning, which helps them make sense of their worlds.

STRENGTHS AND WEAKNESSES OF THE THEORY

The reduced emphasis on prescribed outcomes for learning in the Te Whāriki approach has concerned some critics who have also advocated holistic approaches to learning in young children. Maintaining consistency across practice without learning outcomes being formally agreed may result in significant inconsistencies in practice and in the setting of goals. What appears to be 'good' practice carried out by one practitioner may not be the same for another practitioner. The government in New Zealand has been aware of this and there is ongoing discussion as to the need for more formalized outcomes in learning being adopted. This, however, is likely to create tensions between the original aims and vision of this approach, and new and imposed practice that may be viewed by some as straying away from the key principles of Te Whāriki. Such potential tensions resulting from government were acknowledged some years ago by Miller and Pound (2011, p. 165), who urged caution regarding the influence that governments should have on shaping practice and, particularly, the content and delivery of curricula:

> Such a view would have been anathema to the foundational theorists ... but in England it has become a feature of the Early Years Foundation Stage (EYFS) (DfES, 2008) and the National Curriculum in primary schools, causing uncertainty for many practitioners.

LINKS TO OTHER THEORIES

The Te Whāriki approach has much in common with the underlying principles of other theories and approaches, for example that of Feuerstein and instrumental enrichment, which places enormous emphasis on adults working to facilitate the development of each child's potential through a holistic approach that emphasizes the importance of language and support from adults. These principles are also found in most, if not all, of the theories covered in this text, which go well beyond focusing primarily on attaining skills and acquiring knowledge to exploring the social and emotional needs of children. Like Bronfenbrenner's theoretical approach to learning, the Te Whāriki approach emphasizes the importance of the child's environment, the communities they grow up in and the wider societies of which they become a part.

ACTIVITIES AND POINTS FOR DISCUSSION

Activity: Take time to view the online article: 'Te Whariki – What is this Early Childhood "Curriculum" that ECE Services Are Required by the Ministry of Education to Follow?' by My ECE experts (© 2013–2017): www.myece.org.nz/educational-curriculum-aspects/106-te-whariki-curriculum. Identify the key points in this presentation and then prioritize these in terms of those you consider to be the most important to the least important.

Discussion Point: Do early years settings need to have curricula imposed by government? If so, why, and if not, why not?

EXTENDED AND RECOMMENDED READING

Kanako Murata, K. (2014) *New Zealand Overview and Recent Issues of New Zealand Early Childhood Education Curriculum (Te Whāriki)*. Child Research Net. Available at: www.childresearch.net/projects/ecec/2014_04.html (accessed 05.11.17). (An excellent and comprehensive account of the Te Whāriki approach and recent issues that have presented themselves about this approach.)

REFERENCE

Miller, L. and Pound, L. (2011) *Theories and Approaches to Learning in the Early Years*. London: Sage.

LORIS MALAGUZZI AND REGGIO EMILIA

THE THEORIST (1920–1994)

The Reggio Emilia approach came about largely due to the vision of Loris Malaguzzi, its original founder, who was born in Corregio in Italy. Having studied pedagogy at university, Malaguzzi then began working as a teacher of primary-aged children in 1946, a year after the ending of World War II. Malaguzzi later qualified as an educational psychologist in 1950 and subsequently established the *Psycho-Pedagogical Medical Centre* where he then continued to work for over 20 years. The Reggio Emilia approach first began in the small Italian town of Villa Cella, where, in the turmoil and upset following the end of the war and fascism, local villagers began collecting building materials from the rubble of buildings in the village to build a school. At the time, Malaguzzi visited the village to see what was happening and was so taken by what the villagers were doing and by their motivation that he decided to stay and work in the village as a teacher. Finances for building their first school were raised by the villagers through the sale of a German tank, some trucks and a number of horses. The school remains even today.

KEY PUBLICATION

Malaguzzi, L. (1998) *The Hundred Languages of Children*. Greenwich, CT: Ablex Publishing.

UNDERSTANDING THE THEORY

The origins of the Reggio Emilia approach need to be understood within the context of the time it first emerged. It has been estimated (Lowe, 2013, p. 24) that in the year Malaguzzi started working as a teacher – 1946, there were around 180,000 vagrant children living in the cities of Rome, Naples and Milan, who were 'forced to sleep in doorways and alleys, and kept themselves alive by theft, begging and prostitution'. In the previous summer of 1945, the year the war ended, it has again been estimated by Lowe that some 53,000 'lost children' lived in the city of Berlin. It was against such a backdrop of chaos in Europe that Malaguzzi initiated his ideas on children's learning.

There is no single defined Reggio Emilia approach but rather a number of core principles that inform practice; different schools and settings employ the principles but in varying ways. The Reggio Emilia approach holds that children are born with an innate capacity to develop as individuals and to build their own knowledge of the world around them. Not only are children viewed as having an innate need to interact socially with those

Careful and focused observation of children engaging in activities leads to better understanding of their learning

around them, but they also have the right to do so. It is likely that such an emphasis on children being able to empower themselves through education and learning emanates from the chaos and tragic social conditions that many children in Italy were forced to live in, following World War II.

Central to Malaguzzi's thinking was the importance of observation and documentation of children's learning, with teachers taking photographs of and making regular notes about their pupils' learning, in addition to recording the spoken interactions of the children when collaborating on group activities. Teachers listen carefully to their pupils and document their learning through, for example, books containing their pupils' writing, photographs, pictures, drawings, and so on. In this way, they make the pupils' learning and achievements more visible and tangible and this supports their attempts at evaluating their pupils' learning and progress.

The teachers meet every week to discuss what they have observed and to review the notes they have made on the children's learning. This provides opportunities for discussion and for exploring the individual learning needs and learning styles of their children. These reviews then help with planning the next stages of learning and with shaping activities

over forthcoming weeks. Regular reviews also enable the teachers to gain a better understanding of the holistic needs of their pupils and their ongoing social and emotional development. Teachers are viewed as co-learners and actively collaborate with and alongside their pupils and facilitate new learning through activities that, importantly, focus on the children's interests. Questioning is used as a technique for developing the children's understanding and, importantly, as a way of the teacher being directly involved alongside the children as they learn. In this way, the teacher is almost within the learning situation (Hewett, 2001).

Our environments provide wonderful settings for exploration and learning

A key concept of this approach is that teachers are not trained to follow one type of curriculum and are not bound by working towards tests or externally defined targets; instead, they develop their skills as teachers through, for example, careful observation and interpretation of children's learning behaviours and styles, which in turn inform their curriculum. Teachers are viewed as partners in the learning process alongside their pupils and their pupils' parents. The approach, therefore, is a very flexible one. Malaguzzi also believed strongly in the importance of the environment and how this contributes to and supports children's learning. Through manipulating the environment, teachers can support children in developing and extending their relationships with others in the world around them.

WHAT THE THEORY LOOKS LIKE IN PRACTICE

The curriculum emphasizes creative thinking with much attention given to problem solving and exploration. Longer-term projects are viewed as important in that they provide opportunities for the teacher to work alongside their pupils over time and to be fully involved in the children's learning. Projects commence with the teachers observing the children and questioning them on aspects that are of interest to them. The teachers then introduce materials to support the learning and actively engage the children, through questioning, which then leads to new learning and shapes the project. Malaguzzi used the term 'one hundred languages of children' to refer to how children express their thinking. Teachers support this process through helping children, for example, to express feelings and emotions. The children develop their thinking through using symbols such as their drawings, play and acting, sculpting images, story-telling, speaking and writing. Space and natural light are seen to be as important as indoor plants in terms of easy access to the outdoors. Windows are large and mirrors and displays of children's work are important features of the physical environment. Classrooms have spaces designed for particular activities such as small-group collaborations and the whole school environment is designed in such a way as to provide the children with lots of opportunities to interact with others.

CASE STUDY: THE IMPORTANCE OF ENVIRONMENT

As part of her training to become an early years practitioner, Alana has just commenced working in a local nursery where staff have been very influenced by their recent visit to the Reggio Emilia setting in Italy. Following their return, staff have been very active in placing large mirrors around the setting; Alana is intrigued by how the children take time to observe themselves in these mirrors. She notes how they appear to be paying particular attention to their physical movements and how they can see themselves manipulating the materials they are holding in their hands.

CASE STUDY: WORKING ALONGSIDE CHILDREN AND RECORDING THEIR LEARNING

As part of her training, Alana is also expected to note examples of good practice and report these back to the other students on her degree course when she completes her practice. She observes each day how the staff work alongside groups of children and how they take great care to document their observations of children's learning and how, at the end of the week, they come together to discuss the learning of each child. Over the period of her placement, Alana notes how informed the staff are about each child's learning and what motivates them, and how knowledgeable staff are about the individual holistic needs of each child with whom they work. At the end of her practice, she feeds this back to the other students on her course. She also notes how informed she has become from sitting in on the end-of-week discussions with staff about each child and not only their learning needs but also their social and emotional needs.

STRENGTHS AND WEAKNESSES OF THE THEORY

Given that this approach was created following World War II and the subjugation of many European states by the Nazi regime, it is hardly surprising that substantial significance is placed on the freedom of children to grow and develop in their own right. Children are viewed as individuals and, importantly, much emphasis is placed on the holistic development of each child. The approach has been challenged, however, on the grounds that children are permitted to make errors and to begin learning activities with no clear goals or outcomes.

LINKS TO OTHER THEORIES

Elements of the principles underpinning the Reggio Emilia approach can be found in the theories of Piaget, Vygotsky, Bruner and even Dewey, in that the approach is underpinned by the belief that learning should be a constructive activity. Clearly, this approach, as with that of many of the theorists in this book, places children at the centre of the learning process and emphasizes the importance of individuality and children being seen as having rights and a need to feel confident and in control of their own learning, even from an early age. Like the ideas of Rousseau and Pestalozzi, this approach places great emphasis on children growing up and becoming purposeful and effective citizens who celebrate all that is good about their environments and the societies in which they live.

Children's learning in early years settings reflects the considerable expertise and creativity of practitioners

ACTIVITIES AND POINTS FOR DISCUSSION

Activity: Create a template which practitioners could use as a framework for weekly discussions of children in their educational setting. What key aspects of children's learning would it be necessary to include in the template, in order to gain a clear picture of each child's development that would be meaningful to student practitioners commencing professional practice in a setting?

Discussion Point: Should children in early years settings be encouraged to participate in learning activities where there are no clear goals or outcomes? If so, why, and if not, why not?

EXTENDED AND RECOMMENDED READING

British Association for Early Childhood Education (BAECE) (2012) *Development Matters in the Early Years Foundation Stage (EYFS)*. London: BAECE. (A useful reference source for readers wanting to explore early years practice in the UK.)

Department for Education (DfE) (2014) *Statutory Framework for the Early Years Foundation Stage: Setting the Standards for Learning, Development and Care for Children from Birth to Five*. London: DfE. (A necessary reference source for students against which the principles underpinning Reggio Emilia can be explored.)

Hewitt, V. (2001) 'Examining the Reggio Emilia approach to early childhood education', *Early Childhood Education Journal*, 29(2): 95–100. (An interesting and critical appraisal of this approach.)

Rinaldi, C. (2001) 'A pedagogy of listening: a perspective of listening from Reggio Emilia', *Children in Europe*, 1: 2–5. (A short though interesting study on this approach.)

REFERENCES

Hewett, V. (2001) 'Examining the Reggio Emilia approach to early childhood education', *Early Childhood Education Journal*, 29(2): 95–100.

Lowe, K. (2013) *Savage Continent*. London: Penguin.

PART SUMMARY

Having explored the thinking of theorists and practitioners in the twentieth century who sought to develop the ideas of previous philosophers and thinkers we now turn to an exploration of how their ideas and philosophies fit with practice today. Many of the challenges that faced previous theorists, philosophers and practitioners have now been replaced with new challenges in what is a rapidly changing and interrelated global economic and political context.

PART 3

CHALLENGES FOR THEORISTS IN A CHANGING WORLD

For most children growing up today, early childhood is characterized by a sense of fun, meaningful relationships, regular meals, warmth and security and love. For many, however, this is sadly not the case and there are significant numbers of children who are born into families where few if any of these characteristics are readily apparent (MacBlain, 2014). A particularly worrying feature that continues to adversely affect the lives of so many young children is poverty.

Childhood needs to be a time of emotional growth, exploration and security

THE REALITIES OF CHILDHOOD TODAY

POVERTY

A decade ago, the United Nations General Assembly (UNGA, 2006) drew attention to the significant levels of poverty experienced by children across the globe. The Assembly emphasized how the severe deprivation of materials and basic services adversely affects everyone, but is 'most threatening and harmful to children, leaving them unable to enjoy their rights, to reach their full potential and to participate as full members of society'. Less than a decade ago, Cullis and Hansen (2009, p. 13) indicated how every £100 of additional income in the first nine months of a child's life meant the difference of approximately a month's development by the age of 5 years. Field (2010, p. 28) also drew attention to how 'children from low income families in the UK often grow up to be poor adults ... [they] are more likely to have preschool conduct and behavioural problems'. In a report entitled 'Deprivation and Risk: The Case for Early Intervention' (Action for Children, 2010, p. 12), Dr Ruth Lupton commented on how children from the poorest families in the UK typically begin school with limited vocabularies and with a greater prospect of exhibiting conduct disorders. She stressed how during the primary years at school, children in the UK 'fall further behind', with 'even the brightest children from the most disadvantaged backgrounds' being 'overtaken by the age of 10 by their better-off peers who start off behind them'.

In his annual report, *Unsure Start: HMCI's Early Years Annual Report 2012/13 Speech 2014*, Sir Michael Wilshaw, Her Majesty's Chief Inspector (Ofsted), emphasized how poverty and low-income in families of children in the early years can have a detrimental impact on how children come to realize their future potential and life choices:

> The poorest children are less likely to follow instructions, make themselves understood, manage their own basic hygiene or play well together. By age five, many children have started reading simple words, talking in sentences and can add single numbers. But far fewer of the poorest can do these things well. Children from low-income families are far more likely than their better-off peers to lag behind at age three ... Too

many do badly by the end of primary, and carry on doing badly. (Wilshaw, 2014, p. 3)

It has been recognized (MacBlain, 2014) that, by 6 years of age, children who are intellectually less able and who grow up in rich families are likely to have overtaken intellectually able children growing up in poor families.

POINTS FOR DISCUSSION

View the YouTube video entitled 'BBC World Debate Why Poverty?': www.youtube.com/watch?v=KNIEb3injpc (published on 30 November 2012), hosted by the BBC and 50 other broadcasters around the world, which examines the 'causes' of and 'cures' for the continuing problems underlying severe poverty throughout the world. Then consider:

- How practitioners can gain a better understanding of working with children of different cultural backgrounds where poverty has impacted on their lives.

- (1) The challenges facing families with very young children entering the UK who have experienced extreme poverty; and (2) what early years practitioners might do to support these children in their social and emotional development.

HEALTH

The number of children under the age of 5 who are overweight increased from 32 million across the globe in 1990 to 42 million in 2013. A worrying trend is that most children who are overweight or obese have grown up in developing countries. The World Health Organization (WHO) has estimated that if these trends continue, the number of overweight or obese infants and young children across the globe will increase to 70 million by 2025. The Health and Social Care Information Centre (HSCIC) (2015) reported how in England the number of 4–5-year-olds in their Reception year in 2013/14 who were obese was over 9 per cent. Such statistics are concerning. Overweight and obesity often lead to ill health and, in some cases, to bullying and teasing.

DIVERSITY

The cultural make-up of many early years settings and primary schools in the UK has changed significantly in the last few decades as 'new arrivals' have entered the education system. This has increased in the last few years as migrants escaping conflict in the Middle East have sought to enter Europe. In 2012, the National Association for Language Development in the Curriculum (NALDIC, 2012) reported how the results of the annual School Census in January of that year had indicated that one in six children in primary schools in England did not have English as their first language. NALDIC also drew attention to the fact that more than one in eight children in secondary schools also did not have English as their first language and that these numbers had in fact doubled since 1997.

In the same year, NALDIC (2012) reported that more than one million children in schools in England, aged between 5 and 16 years, were bilingual. In Scotland, the number was over 29,000 and over 31,000 in Wales.

In 2014, the Children and Families Act came into effect in England, followed in 2015 by a new Code of Practice, both of which introduced significant changes to how children with special educational needs should be identified and supported. Of particular note was how the Act and subsequent Code encompassed health with education and social services (see www.gov.uk/government/news/landmark-children-and-families-act-2014-gains-royal-assent for an account of the Act and Code). There has been a significant change in attitude towards children with additional needs over the past few decades, with increasing numbers of children with additional needs being educated in mainstream schools.

EMOTIONAL INTELLIGENCE

It is important for children from their earliest years to understand and manage their own emotions as well as those of others (MacBlain, 2014; MacBlain et al., 2017). By doing so, they come to develop their abilities and skills at engaging purposefully and meaningfully with the world around them and so come to enhance their own learning. This has been referred to as *emotional intelligence* and, in some cases, *emotional literacy* (Goleman, 1996; Salovey and Mayer, 1990). Salovey and Mayer (1990, p. 189) originally defined emotional intelligence as that 'subset of social intelligence that involves the ability to monitor one's own and others' feelings and emotions, to discriminate

Forming secure relationships in the early years enhances future learning

among them and to use this information to guide one's thinking and actions'.

They proposed four factors that are central to how children develop their emotional intelligence, namely: *perceiving*, *reasoning*, *understanding* and *managing* emotions. Children increasingly come to understand their own emotions through attaching meaning to them and forming increasingly accurate interpretations of them. They then learn to regulate their emotions and, through doing so, learn how to manage them. This is important for young children entering early years settings where they are expected to collaborate with others through, for example, taking turns, listening selectively to adults, following instructions and directions, and engaging in activities that might not appeal to them and play. Drawing on the original work of Mayer (co-author with Salovey, referred to earlier), Goleman (1996, p. 48) commented on how Mayer had originally suggested that individuals fall into three distinctive styles when it comes to dealing with their emotions:

- *Self-aware*: here, children, for example, become aware of their own feelings and moods as they occur and don't ruminate or obsess over them.

- *Engulfed*: here, children may be observed typically to feel 'swamped' by their emotions and even 'helpless' in trying to overcome their emotions, with the result that they do little, if anything, to escape their feelings when they feel upset or in a bad mood.

- *Accepting*: here, children typically present as being clear about and accepting of their feelings and don't try to alter them.

Such styles of attending to emotions clearly impact on how children learn to view themselves and, importantly, how in control they feel of their own learning, or what Bandura referred to as 'self-efficacy'.

Recently, Claxton, author of the report 'An Intelligent Look at Emotional Intelligence' (ATL, 2005, p. 20), commissioned by the Association of Teachers and Lecturers, spoke of very young children having an 'emotional apprenticeship', whereby they observe how those around them manage their emotions. Claxton drew an important connection between these observations and learning, suggesting that when infants or toddlers are unsure how to respond

emotionally to someone they have not met before, they 'take their cue from the facial expression and tone of voice of the people they trust – parents obviously, but also … older brothers and sisters'. Claxton goes on to stress how members of a child's family play a significant role in terms of modelling behaviours that steer and direct the child's emotional development, emphasizing how poor modelling can have adverse effects on children: being around an adult who continually 'loses it' is bad for a child's own emotional development.

HOW CHILDREN PLAY

Whilst many aspects of children's play have not changed for generations, much of children's play is now so very different. Less than a decade ago, McDowall Clark (2010, p. 1) drew attention to what is a concerning trend:

> Children do not play out in the street anymore, they are rarely allowed to travel to school on their own … Children spend an increasing proportion of their time in specially designated places such as day nurseries, out-of-school clubs and their own bedrooms, frequently fitted out with the latest technology. Childhood is progressively more regulated so that instead of being a natural part of public life, it takes place in private.

Through play children learn to form and manage relationships

Play is a natural way of learning; it gives meaning to our environments

Physical play develops and strengthens sensory neural pathways in the brain

At the core of much of children's play today can be found a heavy reliance on technology (Beauchamp, 2006, 2012), which can, if overused, bring its own problems. The nature of many of the tensions central to children's play in the UK was brought to the public's attention some years ago by Paton (2012), education editor for the national online UK newspaper *The Telegraph*, when he reported how a number of academics as well as children's authors had written a letter suggesting that controversial education reforms in the UK were 'robbing' children in the early years of 'the ability to play'. In their letter, they also referred to the 'schoolification' of practice in the early years, warning how current revisions of practice were leading to a system that was 'too inflexible' to meet the complex and diverse nature of children's needs in the early years.

The fact that these issues were reported in a national daily newspaper suggests significant concerns regarding the nature of the curricula that young children have access to and the implied absence of play and creativity in their initial years of education. It is now accepted by most, if not all, practitioners that, through play, children learn to communicate and cooperate with others and learn to manage and sustain positive relationships. It is through play that they learn about and understand the world they live in. Play, therefore, is at the very heart of children's thinking and learning and their social and emotional development.

Smith et al. (2003, p. 218) offered a helpful insight into 'play' for young children, suggesting that 'the distinction between exploration and play is difficult to make, as for young infants, all objects are novel'.

They suggest, however, that by the pre-school years this distinction is easier to make. Smith et al. have suggested a conceptual framework through which practitioners can explore the nature of play. They have, for example, proposed three kinds of play: *locomotor*, *sociodramatic* and *language* play. The first involves physical exercise play and what is frequently called rough-and-tumble play. The second refers to play with objects. This might involve fantasy play and/ or play of a sociodramatic nature. The final kind of play has, at its core, language.

LOCOMOTOR PLAY

With this type of play, young children can be observed engaging in physical activities such as rough and tumble, crawling, running and jumping.

Forest School provides enormous opportunities for children to engage in creative learning through natural environments

SOCIODRAMATIC PLAY

Smith et al. (2003) proposed that sociodramatic play may be observed in children as young as 12 months, with the earliest type of pretend play involving behaviours such as children directing actions towards themselves, and their play being at times dependent on the use of objects found in their homes.

LANGUAGE PLAY

This type of play is really 'language' play. Children learn through listening to rhyming poems, riddles, nursery rhymes, and so on, and as they develop they move on to playing games with rules that are

clearly defined structures. Through this final type of play, children learn how to manage relationships and understand the importance of boundaries. Such play offers important opportunities for the developing child to be more active outside of their home and to engage in formal activities and play such as that found at local sports clubs.

FOREST SCHOOL

For many children today, their experience of play can be limited. It is not unusual to hear practitioners talking of the lack of physical play in the lives of some children. This has led many to consider the benefits of play outdoors where children can be introduced to new activities that support learning and develop confidence. This is an area that has been at the centre of many research studies over recent decades. The recognition of those positive aspects offered by Forest School has added significantly to the opportunities that early years practitioners now offer children.

LEARNING AND THE BRAIN

It is astonishing how few books written on the subject of teaching and learning contain any reference to the importance of the brain, yet it is the brain that controls and regulates learning in all children. Central

to our understanding of early brain development is the need to recognize the role that neurons play. Whilst it was once believed that children's brains were complete at birth, it is now known that in addition to the billions of neurons present at birth, the brain continues to generate more neurons throughout life (Gray and MacBlain, 2015). It is whilst the foetus is developing prior to birth that neurons are being formed and form different parts of the brain. As they do so, they establish responses to different chemicals. This process begins with the more primitive areas of the brain such as the brainstem, where those functions that are necessary for bodily development are located. At birth, these functions are fairly well developed and this allows the newly born infant to take in nourishment through, for example, sucking for their mother's milk, breathing, sleeping and hearing and, in general, experiencing sensations in the world around them. After birth, it is the turn of the more advanced areas of the brain to develop, such as the cerebral cortex, which deals with higher order functioning, for example language development, thinking and problem solving. It is during the period following birth and in the early years that most brain development occurs. Different areas of the brain, however, develop their own functions and do so by interacting with chemical agents such as hormones and neurotransmitters.

Following birth, learning continues at an accelerating pace and this involves the strengthening of connections between neurons. Neurons, however, do not make direct contact with each other but have tiny spaces or gaps between them, which are called *synapses*. It is across these spaces or synapses that electrical impulses travel and, as this happens, chemicals known as transmitter substances are released. Hardy and Heyes (1994, pp. 262–3) have drawn attention to the fact that although all messages in the central nervous system are transmitted as nerve impulses, how they are interpreted depends upon that part of the brain that receives them. For example, one part of the brain may interpret the impulse as a sound whilst another part may interpret the impulse as light.

Synapses develop at an extraordinary rate following birth and during the child's first years, and it is because of this that researchers have recognized the importance of stimulating learning in young children during their first months and years. In an infant, the

Following birth, learning continues at an accelerating pace and involves the strengthening of connections between neurons

CASE STUDY: BUILDING STRONG CONNECTIONS IS CRUCIAL TO EARLY LEARNING

George is in his pre-school years and is read to every night after having a warm bath and being put to bed. His parents read him a story in a soft and affirming voice whilst he is cuddled up to them. By doing this, George's parents are ensuring that he will form strong connections within his brain that will be fundamentally different to those of a child who is permitted to remain up late watching television and being spoken to by his parents in monosyllables or being shouted at.

CASE STUDY: ACTIVE LEARNING STRENGTHENS SENSORY NEURAL PATHWAYS

Adam is 3 years of age and is given lots of opportunities to engage in physical play and exercise out of doors. His parents encourage him to climb and develop his physical skills through his play and to take risks. Reuben, on the other hand, spends most of his day and evening watching television whilst sitting on a sofa. As Adam grows older, he presents, unlike Reuben, as a child who is active, has a strong sense of initiative and motivation and is very skilled at sport. Reuben presents as being more passive and less interested in trying new activities, preferring instead to play with his latest digital device.

CASE STUDY: OPPORTUNITIES FOR BUILDING MEMORY START FROM BIRTH

Jude is a very young child who, every evening, is picked up and hugged and tickled by his father when he arrives home from work. Jude gradually constructs a memory of this activity as he learns that when his father lifts him up he will be hugged and tickled and 'loved', and that the experience of being picked up will always be a pleasing experience. If, however, the experience of being lifted by his father has led to him being punished in the past, then he will have internalized the experience of being lifted up as an unpleasant one. It is in such a way that infants' brains serve to help them adapt to the unique environments they are born into, and to others around them. In this way, infants build their understanding of the world in which they live, which might be a nurturing and loving one or one that is not.

part of the brain known as the cerebral cortex may create over a million synapses each second. Though many synapses become established, there are also many that do not and become abandoned by the infant's brain. This process continues throughout life and by adolescence around 50 per cent of synapses have been shed. It is now generally accepted that the brain works on the basis of 'use it or lose it', with many connections between neurons becoming lost if they are not used. The more children engage in play and physical activities and use language, the stronger these connections will be. Now view the YouTube video, 'The Learning Brain', at www.youtube.com/watch?v=cgLYkV689s4, which offers an excellent account of the brain's part in children's learning.

A further important feature of brain development in children is 'myelination' where a 'fatty' substance called myelin acts as an insulator, permitting the transmission of impulses across the synapses. The experiences of infants and particularly the extent of the stimulation they receive in their first months and years can affect the development of myelination and future learning. By the age at which young children are attending pre-school, their brains are almost fully grown in size. Yet another feature of brain development is memory; as infants' experiences are repeated in different situations and over time, the sensory neural pathways that are formed in the brain become more established and go on to form the basis of their memories.

THE EMERGENCE OF DIGITAL LEARNING

The digital presence in children's lives frequently commences even before birth when, for example, expectant mothers and fathers show to friends and relatives ultrasound images of their babies and even post these images on social media

Digital technology can offer new and exciting ways of learning

sites (Leaver, 2015). Children's digital footprints then typically commence following birth (MacBlain et al., 2017), with perhaps the majority of children growing up in homes where they come into daily contact with a whole range of digital devices. Indeed, most children are now introduced to digital technology soon after birth (Chaudron, 2015). In effect, even the youngest of children today become quickly immersed in home environments that are characterized, and in many cases defined, by a growing reliance on technology (Teichert and Anderson, 2014).

Even before children are born, they have become part of the 'app generation' (Gardner and Davis, 2013). Many mothers now use apps when they become pregnant, as is demonstrated by the following case of the mother of a young baby:

> Fiona: I used an app that equates to the size of the foetus – it will give you a weekly update on the development of the foetus; it equates to the size of a strawberry or a lemon, it helps you imagine. Wonderweeks!

By the age of 2, for example, children can be observed to be using tablets or computers. It has been estimated (ChildWise, 2015) that over 40 per cent of children in the UK use these every day. In a recent UK report, which focused on play and creative learning in the use of apps by pre-schoolers, it was acknowledged that 65 per cent of 3–7-year-olds had access to a tablet computer at home, with parents reporting how children under the age of 5 used tablet computers on average for over an hour on a typical weekday (Marsh et al., 2015). Many young children now use tablet computers almost as second nature and can be observed tapping and swiping the screens of these devices with confidence and ease. McTavish (2014, p. 320) emphasized how many adults can find it a challenge to use technology within their lives, whereas for children it has become their normal life experience.

It is also now generally recognized that young children do not limit their game playing to tablet computers but increasingly also use smartphones. Chaudron (2015) has drawn attention to how young children also use smartphones to watch videos, play games, send messages, take pictures, and make video calls and phone calls. This is a practice that is often permitted and even encouraged by parents, with very young children typically using smartphones belonging to their parents or older siblings. Recently, ChildWise (2015), for example, reported that some 35 per cent of pre-school children had used a parent's phone.

Technology can offer opportunities for developing independent learning

> ### POINT FOR DISCUSSION
>
> View the YouTube video entitled 'Katie Davis and The App Generation at Town Hall': www.youtube.com/watch?v=_uRNrGAYEMM. Then consider:
>
> - How digital technology is changing the lives of young children. Are young children, for example, increasingly learning to expect immediate answers to their questions? Do children communicate more with their parents than in previous decades by using mobile phones? Are young children increasingly defining themselves through the 'brands' that are being made available to them?

DIGITAL TECHNOLOGY IN THE CLASSROOM

Children now enter early childhood settings having already had access to a wide range of digital technology within their homes. Used properly, these devices can offer excellent learning opportunities. Flewitt et al. (2015) have emphasized how the absence of more innovative attempts at using digital technologies in classrooms and early years settings may work against children having important opportunities for learning. Neumann and Neumann (2014), for example, have drawn attention to how tablet computers emulate many of the features of books and provide excellent and exciting opportunities for literacy development. Screens can now look like the pages of books and children can, with the swipe of a finger, turn over pages and enlarge pictures and visual details that capture their interest. A variety of apps geared to helping children create their own stories now even allow children to build in pictures and sounds, which make them more visually appealing and add to their motivation to read and explore ideas in greater detail. In this way, children can be encouraged to be more creative in their literacy activities (Kucirkova and Sakr, 2015).

> ### POINT FOR DISCUSSION
>
> Consider how early years practitioners might work with parents to guide and support them in using digital technology as a learning opportunity with their children.

DIGITAL TECHNOLOGY IN THE HOME

Many young children are now engaging with digital technologies as parents provide their children with opportunities to do so and as working patterns have changed over recent decades where both parents are now often working full-time (MacBlain, 2014). Evans (2014) has emphasized how young people previously explored and experimented with shaping and understanding their identities through going out into the worlds around them, through exploration of their physical worlds. Children today can engage in this process from the comfort of their own homes and bedrooms. In the last few decades, many parents have invested in digital technology, buying computers, tablets and smartphones and paying for access to the internet with the belief that

The journey begins

this will benefit their children's education and learning. Ownership of digital technology is now often viewed as a sign of good parenting, where some parents may downplay the social aspect of digital technology in favour of its educational uses (Willett, 2015).

DIGITAL TECHNOLOGY: HIDDEN CHALLENGES

A recent report by the ONS (2015), which focused on children's mental health and well-being in the UK, emphasized how children who spend over three hours each day on social media sites are over twice as likely to experience poor mental health. There are of course hidden risks such as cyber-bullying and child pornography that can have a devastating impact on children (Binford, 2015).

ACTIVITY

Look at the website 'Internet Matters' (www.internetmatters.org) and then consider what you have learned from different internet sources about children's learning.

PART SUMMARY

Most children today have positive and rewarding experiences in early childhood. There are many, however, who, sadly, do not and require much greater support from adults outside of their homes. Early years practitioners are in a unique position to play a key role in supporting children, not only with their learning but also with their social and emotional development, not to mention their physical growth. Practitioners who work to fully understand their children's individual needs daily enjoy the rewards of seeing children develop. They are also there at times when children need emotional support and security, where, for example, they are experiencing situations and problems they may not even begin to comprehend. Being a practitioner in an early years setting is surely one of the most rewarding and satisfying jobs.

EXTENDED AND RECOMMENDED READING

Flewitt, R., Messer, D. and Kucirkova, N. (2015) 'New directions for early literacy in a digital age: the iPad', *Journal of Early Childhood Literacy*, 15(3): 289–310. (An interesting and informative account regarding the use of iPads by children in their acquisition of early literacy.)

Wohlwend, K. (2015) 'Making, remaking and reimaging the everyday: play, creativity and popular media', in J. Rowsell and K. Pahl (eds), *Routledge Handbook of Literacy Studies* (pp. 548–60). London: Routledge. (A useful text that links children's creativity and play with popular media and literacy.)

www.forestschoolassociation.org/the-forest-school-association – a link to the Forest School Association, providing a great deal of useful information as well as giving an excellent overview of the FS concept.

REFERENCES

Action for Children (2010) *Deprivation and Risk: The Case for Early Intervention*. London: Action for Children.

Association of Teachers and Lecturers (ATL) (2005) *An Intelligent Look at Emotional Intelligence*. London: ATL.

Beauchamp, G. (2006) 'New technologies and "new teaching": a process of evolution?', in R. Webb (ed.), *Changing Teaching and Learning in the Primary School*. Maidenhead: Open University Press.

Beauchamp, G. (2012) *ICT in the Primary School: From Pedagogy to Practice*. London: Pearson.

Binford, W. (2015) *The Digital Child*. Social Science Research Network. Available at: http://ssrn.com/abstract=2563874 (accessed 06.11.2017).

Chaudron, S. (2015) *Young Children (0–8) and Digital Technology: A Qualitative Exploratory Study across Seven Countries*. Luxembourg: Publications Office of the European Union.

ChildWise (2015) *The Monitor Pre-School Report: Key Behaviour Patterns Among 0–4 Year Olds.* London: ChildWise.

Cullis, A. and Hansen, K. (2009) *Child Development in the First Three Sweeps of the Millenium Cohort Study*. DCSF Research Report RW-007. London: DCSF.

Evans, S. (2014) 'The challenge and potential of the digital age: young people and the internet', *Transactional Analysis Journal*, 44(2): 153–66.

Field, F. (2010) *The Foundation Years: Preventing Poor Children Becoming Poor Adults – Report of the Independent Review on Poverty and Life Chances*. London: Cabinet Office.

Flewitt, R., Messer, D. and Kucirkova, N. (2015) 'New directions for early literacy in a digital age: the iPad', *Journal of Early Childhood Literacy*, 15(3): 289–310.

Gardner, H. and Davis, K. (2013) *The App Generation*. London: Yale University Press.

Goleman, D. (1996) *Emotional Intelligence: Why It Can Matter More than IQ*. London: Bloomsbury.

Gray, C. and MacBlain, S.F. (2015) *Learning Theories in Childhood* (2nd edn). London: Sage.

Hardy, M. and Heyes, S. (1994) *Beginning Psychology: A Comprehensive Introduction to Psychology* (4th edn). Oxford: Oxford University Press.

Health and Social Care Information Centre (HSCIC) (2015) Statistics on Obesity, Physical Activity and Diet: England 2015. Available at: https://digital.nhs.uk/catalogue/PUB16988 (accessed 20.10.17).

Kucirkova, N. and Sakr, M. (2015) 'Child–father creative text-making at home with crayons, iPad collage and PC', *Thinking Skills and Creativity*, 17: 59–73.

Leaver, T. (2015) 'Researching the ends of identity: birth and death on social media', *Social Media +*

Society, May [online]. Available at: http://journals.sagepub.com/doi/full/10.1177/2056305115578877 (accessed 13.10.17).

MacBlain, S.F. (2014) *How Children Learn*. London: Sage.

MacBlain, S.F., Dunn, J. and Luke, I. (2017) *Contemporary Childhood*. London: Sage.

McDowall Clark, R. (2010) *Childhood in Society: For Early Childhood Studies*. Exeter: Learning Matters.

McTavish, M. (2014) '"I'll do it my way!": a young child's appropriation and recontextualization of school literacy practices in out-of-school spaces', *Journal of Early Childhood Literacy*, 14(3): 319–44.

Marsh, J., Plowman, L., Yamada-Rice, D., Bishop, J.C., Lahmar, J., Scott, F., et al. (2015) Exploring Play and Creativity in Pre-schoolers' Use of Apps: Report for Early Years Practitioners. Available at: www.techandplay.org/reports/TAP_Final_Report.pdf (accessed 20.10.17).

National Association for Language Development in the Curriculum (NALDIC) (2012) Research and Information. Available at: www.naldic.org.uk/research-and-information/eal-statistics (accessed 20.10.17).

Neumann, M. and Neumann, D. (2014) 'Touch screen tablets and emergent literacy', *Early Childhood Education Journal*, 42: 231–9.

Office for National Statistics (ONS) (2015) Measuring National Well-being: Insights into Children's Mental Health and Well-being. Available at: www.ons.gov.uk/peoplepopulationandcommunity/wellbeing/articles/measuringnationalwellbeing/2015-10-20 (accessed 03.01.18).

Paton, G. (2012) 'New-style "nappy curriculum" will damage childhood', *The Telegraph*, 6 February. Available at: www.telegraph.co.uk/education/educationnews/9064870/New-style-nappy-curriculum-will-damage-childhood.html (accessed 28.01.15).

Salovey, P. and Mayer, J.D. (1990) 'Emotional intelligence', *Imagination, Cognition, and Personality*, 9: 185–211.

Smith, K.S., Cowie, H. and Blades, M. (2003) *Understanding Children's Development* (4th edn). Oxford: Blackwell.

Teichert, L. and Anderson, A. (2014) '"I don't even know what blogging is": the role of digital media in a five-year-old girl's life', *Early Child Development and Care*, 184(11): 1677–91.

United Nations General Assembly (UNGA) (2006) *Promotion and Protection of the Rights of Children: Report of the Third Committee*. New York: United Nations.

Willett, R.J. (2015) 'The discursive construction of "good parenting" and digital media: the case of children's virtual world games', *Media, Culture and Society*, 37(7): 1060–75.

Wilshaw, W. (2014) *Unsure Start: HMCI's Early Years Annual Report 2012/13*. London: Ofsted. Contains public sector information licensed under the Open Government Licence v3.0: www.nationalarchives.gov. uk/doc/open-government-licence/version/3 (accessed 03.11.17).

INDEX